Helion & Company Limited
Unit 8 Amherst Business Centre
Budbrooke Road
Warwick
CV34 5WE
England
Tel. 01926 499 619
Email: info@helion.co.uk
Website: www.helion.co.uk
Twitter: @helionbooks
Visit our blog http://blog.helion.co.uk/

Text © Adrien Fontanellaz, Tom Cooper and
    José Augusto Matos 2020
Colour profiles © David Bocquelet, Luca
    Canossa and Tom Cooper 2020
Maps © Tom Cooper 2020
Photographs © as individually credited

Designed & typeset by Farr out Publications,
    Wokingham, Berkshire
Cover design by Paul Hewitt, Battlefield
    Design (www.battlefield-design.co.uk)
Printed for Helion & Co by Henry Ling Ltd.,
    Dorchester, Dorset

ISBN 978-1-913118-61-7

British Library Cataloguing-in-Publication
    Data
A catalogue record for this book is available
    from the British Library

We always welcome receiving book
proposals from prospective authors.

Contents

Note: To simplify the use of this book, all names, locations and geographic designations
are as provided in *The Times World Atlas*, or other traditional accepted major sources of
reference, as of the time of described events. For example, the modern-day Republic
of Namibia is usually cited as South West Africa (SWA) because that designation for
this territory remained in use in the English language while it was under South African
administration from 1915 until 1990 - despite the decision of the United Nations General
Assembly from 1968, which changed its designation to Namibia. When mentioned
for the first time in the text, aircraft and heavy weapons system designations are cited
fully – including their designer and/or the manufacturer, official military designation
and nickname: in the case of Soviet-made armament: this is followed by the ASCC/
NATO-codename, which is then also used through the text. The same principle is applied
to Angolan and Cuban military terminology, the most important details of which are
provided in Table 1.

Abbreviations

AB	air base
AM	Aeródromo de Manobras (manoeuvre aerodrome)
ANC	African National Congress (South Africa)
APC	armoured personnel carrier
ASCC	Air Standardisation Coordinating Committee (US, UK, Australian and New Zealand committee for standardisation of designations for foreign (primarily Soviet) armament; its codenames were subsequently adopted by NATO, and are commonly known as 'NATO designations')
ATGM	anti-tank guided missile
BOSS	Bureau for State Security (South Africa)
C3	command, control, and communication
CAP	combat air patrol
CAS	close air support
CIA	Central Intelligence Agency (USA)
c/n	construction number
CO	Commanding Officer
COIN	counterinsurgency
DAA/FAR	Defensa Antiaérea y Fuerza Aérea Revolucionaria (Revolutionary Air Defence and Air Force, Cuba)
DRC	Democratic Republic of the Congo (Congo-Kinshasa, also Zaire)
DTA	Direccao dos Transportes Aéros (Portuguese civilian Aviation company)
ECM	electronic countermeasures
ELNA	Exército de Libertação Nacional de Angola (Angola National Liberation Army), FNLA armed wing
FAC	forward air controller
FALA	Forças Armadas de Libertação de Angola (Angola Liberation Armed Forces; armed wing of UNITA)
FAP	Força Aérea Portuguesa (Portuguese Air Force)
FAPA/DAA	Força Aérea Popular de Angola/Defesa Anti-Aérea (Angola People's Air Force and Anti-Aircraft Defence)
FAPLA	Forças Armadas Populares de Libertação de Angola (People's Armed Forces of Liberation of Angola)
FAR	Fuerzas Armadas Revolucionarias (Revolutionary Armed Forces, of Cuba)
FAZ	Forces Armées Zaïroises (Zairian Armed Forces)
FLEC	Frente para a Libertação do Enclave de Cabinda (Front for the Liberation of the Enclave of Cabinda, Angola)
FNLA	Frente Nacional de Libertação de Angola (Angola National Liberation Front)
FNLC	Front National pour la Libération du Congo (National Front for the Liberation of the Congo)
FOB	Forward Operating Base
GenStab	General Staff (of the armed forces of the USSR, equivalent to the Joint Chiefs of Staff in the USA)
GVS	glavnyi voennyi sovetnik (Russian for 'Chief Military Advisor')
HQ	headquarters
IFV	infantry fighting vehicle
INS	instrumental navigation system
IRST	infra-red search and track (system)
MANPAD	man-portable air defence (system)
MBT	main battle tank
MGPA	Marinha de Guerra Popular de Angola (The People's Navy of Angola)
MGR	Marina de Guerra Revolucionaria (Revolutionary Navy, Cuba)
MiG	Mikoyan i Gurevich (the design bureau led by Artyom Ivanovich Mikoyan and Mikhail Iosifovich Gurevich, also known as OKB-155 or MMZ' "Zenit")
MINFAR	Ministerio de las Fuerzas Armadas Revolucionarias (Ministry of the Revolutionary Armed Forces, Cuba)
MININT	Ministerio del Interior (Ministry of Interior, Cuba)
MMCA	Misión Militar de Cuba en Angola (Cuban Military Mission in Angola)
MPLA	Movimento Popular de Libertacao de Angola (People's Movement for the Liberation of Angola)
MRL	multiple rocket launcher
NATO	North Atlantic Treaty Organisation
NCO	non-commissioned officer
NGO	non-governmental organisation
ODP	Organizção de Defeza Popular (People's Defence Organisation: MPLA/FAPLA-controlled militia)
PLAN	People's Liberation Army of Namibia (SWAPO's armed wing)
PRC	People's Republic of China (or mainland China)
RPG	rocket-propelled grenade (launcher)
RSA	Republic of South Africa
SAAF	South African Air Force
SADF	South African Defence Forces
SA-2 Guideline	ASCC/NATO-codename for Soviet S-75 Dvina SAM-system
SA-3 Goa	ASCC/NATO-codename for Soviet S-125 Pechora SAM-system
SA-6 Gainful	ASCC/NATO-codename for Soviet ZRK-SD Kub/Kvadrat SAM-system
SA-7a Grail	ASCC/NATO-codename for Soviet 9K32 Strela-2 MANPAD
SA-7b Grail	ASCC/NATO-codename for Soviet 9K92M Strela-2M MANPAD
SA-8 Gecko	ASCC/NATO-codename for Soviet 9K33 Osa SAM-system
SA-9 Gaskin	ASCC/NATO-codename for Soviet ZRK-BD Strela-1 SAM-system
SA-13 Gopher	ASCC/NATO-codename for Soviet ZRK-BD Strela-10 SAM-system
SA-14 Gremlin	ASCC/NATO-codename for Soviet 9M36 Strela-3 MANPAD

SA-16 Gimlet	ASCC/NATO-codename for Soviet 9M313 Igla-1 MANPAD
SA-18 Grouse	ASCC/NATO-codename for Soviet 9M39 Igla MANPAD
SAR	search and rescue
SARH	semi-active radar homing (type of guided air-to-air missile)
SDECE	Service de Documentation Extérieure et de Contre-Espionage (External Documentation and Counter-Espionage Service, France)
Shilka	Nick-name for Soviet ZSU-23-4 self-propelled, radar-equipped anti-aircraft gun
SMMA	Soviet Military Mission in Angola
SWA	South West Africa (present day Namibia)
SWAPO	South West African People's Organisation (insurgency in the former South West Africa)
TAAG	Transportes Aéreos Angolanos (Angolan Air Transport, later TAAG, Angola Airlines)

TEL	transporter-erector-launcher
UAV	unmanned aerial vehicle
UNITA	União Nacional para a Independência Total de Angola (National Union for the Total Independence of Angola)
UNIMOG	UNIversal-MOtor-Gerät (range of multi-purpose, all-wheel-drive trucks manufactured by Daimler and sold under Mercedes Benz)
USA	United States of America
USSR	Union of Soviet Socialist Republics (Soviet Union)
VDV	vozdushno-desantnye voyska (Russian for airborne troops)
VTA	Voyenno-Transportnaya Aviatsiya (Soviet Air Force's Military Transport Aviation)
VVS	Voyenno-Vozdushnye Sily (Soviet Air Force)
Volga	S-75, Soviet radar-guided surface-to-air system, ASCC/NATO-codename 'SA-2 Guideline'

Introduction

Preparing this book was a long and often laborious process. The original idea was born over a dozen years ago. During the work on the project *African MiGs* – a book summarising the operational history of MiG and Sukhoi designed jet fighters with 23 air forces of Sub-Saharan Africa – the authors established contact with Teniente-Coronel Eduardo Gonzalez Sarria, a retired fighter pilot and squadron commander of the Revolutionary Air Defence and Air Force of Cuba (Defensa Antiaérea y Fuerza Aérea Revolucionaria, DAA/FAR).[1] While that link enabled the provision of unprecedentedly precise information about the DAA/FAR's operations in Angola during the 1980s, lots of additional information from Angolan sources became available after its publication, making it obvious that another, dedicated book would be necessary to provide a detailed study of the operational history of the FAPA/DAA. Sadly, many subsequent developments prevented the realisation of this idea at the time. Negative experiences with Cuban authorities at home, and with publishers abroad, eventually discouraged Teniente-Coronel Gonzalez from continuing our cooperation. Moreover, geographic distances, language barriers, lack of first-hand contacts, documentation, and illustrations, and preoccupation with other projects kept the authors away from realising the idea of a separate book on the Angolan and Cuban air forces during what is generally known as the 'Angolan Civil War' or 'II Angolan War' in the West, and the 'War of Intervention' in Angola, which was fought between 1975 and 1992.

A new attempt was launched simultaneously with the decision to prepare the *War of Intervention in Angola* mini-series as a part of Helion's Africa@War project, about four years ago. Eventually, following extensive studies of the available information, we took the decision to 'integrate' the coverage of the DAA/FAR and the FAPA/DAA into the third and fourth volumes of this mini-series. This resulted in what might be seen as an unusual composition for this volume: its first part rolls out the history of the Angolan air force from its beginnings up to around 1983 in – for the English language – unprecedented detail. The second part then offers an integrated narrative on subsequent air and land operations. One reason is that aerial warfare is one of the hardest military disciplines to quantify

and qualify, and one which never takes place entirely on its own or in a sort of vacuum: it is always related to developments on the ground and to geo-strategic and socio-economic affairs. Another reason is related to the unique organisation, structure and equipment of what used to be the armed forces of the USSR: both the DAA/FAR and then the FAPA/DAA were originally organised, trained, equipped and indoctrinated in what can be described as the 'Soviet style'. This is likely to appear perfectly logical to most of the readers in the West, and particularly those studying Soviet military thought of the 1970s and the 1980s, at the time the General Staff of the Soviet Armed Forces was completely preoccupied with equipping and training the Soviet forces for an all-out war with those of NATO, foremost in Europe. It is likely to appear that way to most readers in South Africa too, where the opinion remains widespread that what is variously called the 'Bush War' or the 'Border War' of the 1980s was an element of the Cold War, provoked by attempt of the Communist-block – and the USSR in particular – to 'encroach' upon the Republic of South Africa (RSA). On the other hand, the same narrative is likely to appear 'factually incorrect' to a number of readers in Angola and Cuba, not to mention readers of younger generations. The reason is not only that neither Angola nor the fourth involved party – the former South West Africa (SWA), which then became Namibia – have subsequently pursued the development of Communism/Marxism/Leninism – but that both the DAA/FAR and then the FAPA/DAA gradually went their own way and developed their own strategy and tactics: indeed, that for much of the 1980s there was a major dispute between the leaders in Havana and Luanda, and those in Moscow over the issue of how to conduct the war against the insurgency of the National Union for the Total Independence of Angola (União Nacional para a Independência Total de Angola, UNITA), and against the South African Defence Force (SADF) in Angola.

Obviously, not only does each of the involved parties in a conflict as complex as this one have its own 'official line', but also every participant and every eyewitness has his or her own recollections and point of view, and the same is valid for those striving to record the history. However, what this book is going to show is that both the DAA/FAR and the FAPA/DAA remained heavily influenced by Soviet military thinking throughout the war in Angola of the 1980s – if for no other reason than because the mass of their equipment was Soviet-designed and manufactured, and thus came together with very specific limitations. In turn, precisely the limitations of the Soviet-designed weapon systems are both a much understudied and a heavily misunderstood issue – in the West and in South Africa. On the other hand, training of Angolan military personnel in the USSR that was too conservative, too slow, too unrealistic and thus poor, aggravated these limitations. Precisely this mix of factors has heavily influenced the final shape and content of this volume.

That all said, this work is not meant to judge anything or anybody but should be read as an attempt to record what is known, to understand it and to explain it. As historians, we have no axes to grind, but are curious to research air forces, aircraft and aerial warfare and this also requires the studying, understanding – and explaining – of a host of geo-strategic issues.

For the work on this project, the authors are heavily indebted to many individuals for their help. Among those we wish to thank

are Albert Grandolini, from France, who helped with the provision of much advice and information, and his extensive photo-library; Martin Smisek, from the Czech Republic, who helped with information obtained during his research in local military archives; Adrian Roman, from Romania, who has selflessly shared the results of his research about the Romanian involvement in Angola; Greg Swart, from South Africa, who provided intricate details on specific Angolan and Cuban-flown aircraft; and to Fausto Biloslavo, from Italy, and Al J Venter, from South Africa, who have both kindly provided photographs taken during often months-long travels around Angola. In addition to our families, who have been especially understanding during a period of intensive work, we would also like to express our gratitude to a number of people who have contributed 'bits and pieces' of information over time, including (in alphabetic order), Humberto Campos Abranttes, Chris Botha, Herve Desallier, Alexander Golz, Alexander Guk, Tom Long, William Marshal, Marco Moutinho, Carlos Oliveira, Antoine Pierre, Alvaro Ponte, Chris Thornburg, Claudio Tosselli, Steve Touchdown, Pit Weinert, and Ben Wilhelmi.

1

Who-was-Whom in Angola, 1975-1985

The War in Angola of the 1980s was an extremely complex affair, involving multiple nationalist movements, and an even higher number of foreign powers. For the reader's easier understanding of the subsequent narrative, the following chapter will provide a brief introduction to all of the involved parties and their strategic aims.

The End of Portuguese Rule

The I Angolan War, or the Angolan War of Independence, erupted with a series of uprisings against Portuguese colonial rule in 1961. During the following years, three major nationalist insurgent movements and one separatist movement crystallised:

People's Movement for the Liberation of Angola (Movimento Popular de Libertação de Angola, MPLA), led by Agostinho Neto. It primarily consisted of the Mbundu ethnic group, and was thus representative of a large segment of the native population living along the coast of the Atlantic Ocean. In 1975, the MPLA's armed wing became the People's Armed Forces of Liberation of Angola (Forças Armadas Populares de Libertação de Angola, FAPLA) – the regular Angolan armed forces.

Angolan National Liberation Front (Frente Nacional de Libertação de Angola, FNLA), led by Holden Roberto, exclusively consisted of the BaKongo ethnic group of northern Angola, and including its armed wing, the Angolan National Liberation Army (Exército de Libertação Nacional de Angola, ELNA);

National Union for the Total Independence of Angola Angola (União Nacional para a Independência Total de Angola, UNITA), led by Jonas Savimbi, primarily consisted of the Ovimbundu ethnic group from southern and eastern Angola, and included its own armed wing, the Angola Liberation Armed Forces (Forças Armadas de Libertação de Angola, FALA);

Front for the Liberation of the Enclave of Cabinda (Frente para a Libertacao do Enclave de Cabinda, FLEC), was led by Henriques Tiago, and sought independence for the Cabinda Enclave, which the Portuguese eventually granted to Angola.

While widely described as communist, the MPLA followed a leftist nationalist ideology but received very little help from the USSR and the People's Republic of China (PRC) during the 1960s; subsequently, it was supported by Algeria, Yugoslavia, and a few other African nations. The FNLA invested next to nothing into ideological work, and was supported by neighbouring Democratic Republic of Zaire (official designation of what was the Democratic Republic of the Congo, from 1960 until 1971, and again since 1997), and, from early 1975, by the USA. UNITA was supported by the PRC. Representative of a part of the population of the Cabinda Enclave, the FLEC played no important role in the creation of Angola.[2]

The Portuguese brought under control all three movements in the course of their military campaigns of 1972-1973 and forced most of them out of Angola. However, a military coup in Lisbon on 25 April 1974 – known as the Carnation Revolution – brought to power a government that decided to end the colonial wars, and release Angola, along with Portuguese Guiné and Mozambique, into independence. Indeed, the Portuguese quickly agreed cease-fires with the FNLA, the MPLA, and UNITA and left them establish their representatives in Luanda in October 1974. The MPLA, enjoying the support of most of the population, then won a short but bitter civil war against the FNLA and UNITA, and de-facto imposed itself as the future government of Angola, which officially achieved independence on 11 November 1975.

Operation Carlota

From late 1974, the MPLA began receiving military support from Cuba, provided via the neighbouring state of Congo-Brazzaville. Subsequently, the Cubans began delivering an increasing amount

Two officers assigned to the MMCA in 1976. Notable are their 'colourful' uniforms and a mix of firearms, including not only an assault rifle from the AK-47-series (left), but also an Israeli-made Uzi sub machine gun, almost certainly captured from one of the mercenary groups supported by the USA and France. (via Luis Dominguez)

of their aid directly to Luanda. When Angola officially became independent, on 11 November 1975, and acting under the UN Charter, Cuba launched an 'intervention on invitation', Operation Carlota: this resulted in the deployment of around 36,000 officers and other ranks of the Revolutionary Armed Forces of Cuba (Fuerzas Armadas Revolucionarias, FAR) – including a sizeable contingent of the DAA/FAR – by March 1976. While the I Angolan War or the Angolan War of Independence of 1961-1975 thus ended, a new conflict, the II Angolan War erupted, and was to last until 1992.

Officially, all of the Cuban military personnel in Angola were assigned to the Cuban Military Mission in Angola (Misión Militar de Cuba en Angola, MMCA). The original – and official – purpose of the MMCA was not to fight, but to remain 'limited': to advise and support the MPLA and the FAPLA. However, due to the lack of the native cadre, and the necessity to train dozens of thousands of Angolans, the MMCA found itself not only commanding and controlling the FAPLA for most of the mid-1970s, but also fighting for it. Indeed, all the major campaigns of 1976 saw large contingents of the MMCA literally 'embedded' into FAPLA units. In turn, the Cuban involvement on such a scale eventually encouraged the Soviet leadership in Moscow to start selling arms and providing advisors to Angola. By early 1976, about 500 of these were present in the country, organised into the Soviet Military Mission in Angola (SMMA).

MPLA's First Victory

Supported by Zaire, the USA (via the CIA), and France, and reinforced by a sizeable group of European mercenaries (including Portuguese veterans of the colonial armed forces), the FNLA invaded northern Angola and launched an advance on Luanda in October 1975. However, this effort was defeated in the Battle of Quifangondo, on 10 November. Moreover, through December 1975, and January-March 1976, the MMCA and FAPLA then ran a series of offensives driving the surviving FNLA-insurgents and mercenaries into Zaire. Around the same time, the MMCA and FAPLA also defeated the Zairian-supported FLEC in the Cabinda Enclave.

Meanwhile, encouraged by Western powers, and in support of UNITA, South Africa launched its own intervention in Angola – Operation Savannah – securing the entire southern part of the country and much of the centre. However, the closer the SADF moved to Luanda, the more stubborn the resistance of the MMCA and the FAPLA became. Ultimately, the MPLA secured power in Luanda and the RSA was left without a choice but to withdraw completely. In its wake, the Cubans and the Angolans defeated UNITA, and by June 1976 secured more than 90% of the country.

Colonel Alberto Colome Ibarra (centre, with glasses) – the first commander of one of FAR brigades deployed in Angola of 1975 – and his staff, seen observing the battlefield. (Albert Grandolini Collection)

Moscow's Position

Although countless Western accounts have superimposed the USSR's role in Angola to a degree where the Cuban Operation Carlota is frequently misinterpreted as undertaken on order from Moscow, the truth is that the Soviet leadership was primarily keen to maintain the status quo and not to provoke the West. As confirmed by official Cuban documentation released in recent years, even Yugoslavia and Algeria – two officially non-aligned, but Soviet-friendly countries – failed in their efforts to convince the Soviet leadership to support the MPLA in 1974-1975. One might oversimplify this by concluding that as well-educated and convinced Marxists – at least in theory – the Soviets knew all too well that it would take a well-developed and industrialised economy to create communism, and thus no similar development was possible in Angola, a country where almost the entire population was illiterate. In similar fashion, the Cubans of the time could have been described as 'true idealists': the only factor important to their leadership was the 'revolutionary spirit' of the people eager to attract their support. However, as of early 1975, Moscow entirely committed itself to the success of a summit with the US government in Helsinki, Finland, where it hoped to obtain formal recognition of the status quo in Europe. Correspondingly, its direct intervention in Angola was out of the question. Instead, an intervention through Cuba limited the risks: indeed, in the case of a direct confrontation with the USA, and especially in the case of a failure or a possible ultimatum from Washington, the visibility of Cuba's involvement would save the Soviets from a similar humiliation to that of the Cuban Crisis. Finally, the Organisation of African Unity (OAU) was insistent on keeping great powers out of local conflicts in Africa, and numerous African governments – including Soviet allies – expressed their position in this regard: this was something even Moscow could not ignore.[3] Thus, it fell on Fidel Castro, once he convinced himself of the MPLA's 'progressive' ideology, to launch a military intervention – essentially, on his own, and contrary to Soviet interests. Unsurprisingly, the Soviets became involved rather reluctantly: even once the MMCA's and FAPLA's operations had secured nearly all of Angola, they foremost concentrated on influencing the new government and its ideology.

Differences in Military Thinking

Differences between the Cubans and the Soviets were not limited to politics: they were at least as significant on the military level. As discussed in *Volume 1* of this mini-series, as of the mid-1970s, the Cubans were still fresh from fighting an extensive counterinsurgency (COIN) campaign at home, and from supervising the establishment and build-up of nearly a dozen armed forces around Africa and the Middle East. As well as possessing recent combat experience from multiple 'local wars', they also had a much shorter chain of command than the Soviets: therefore, the experiences of their field commanders had had a much more direct impact upon the decisions of their political leadership than was ever the case in the USSR. Unsurprisingly, the Cubans recognised numerous flaws in Soviet military thinking and began training their troops and operating in a different fashion: they envisaged improved training of junior commanders and understood air power as a crucial factor for ground operations. From the Western point of view, it can be said that they began emphasising flexibility, and quality over quantity.[4]

On the contrary, in the USSR of the early-to-mid-1970s, the central role at the strategic and operational level was played by the General Staff of the Soviet Armed Forces (GenStab or GenShtab): this was (and remains in the Russian Federation today) its own branch of the armed forces, staffed by a caste of professional military thinkers. The GenStab was responsible for all planning at strategic and operational levels, the development of doctrine and capabilities of all branches of the armed forces, and acted as the sole procurement authority in the USSR for the strategic forces, air defence forces, army, air force, and the navy alike. The worst case scenario for which the GenStab was preparing the Soviet armed forces was one of an all-out nuclear war against NATO. Correspondingly, it organised, equipped and trained the Soviet armed forces for exactly that kind of war. With a handful of exceptions, the Soviets possessed no combat experience since the Second World War: the few ideas they had had about modern-day warfare were all based on ideologically-smudged reporting about the Vietnam War, fought between the USA and North Vietnam, from 1961 until 1973. Therefore, the GenStab based the majority of its assessments and estimates on the experiences from the Second World War.[5]

Following that method of thinking, the role of air power was that of 'extended-range artillery': the provision of fire-support for ground forces along the frontlines and to a maximum depth of around 100 kilometres (62 miles) beyond: it was unthinkable to deploy air power in strategic or operational level campaigns. Correspondingly, while administratively an independent branch of the armed forces, at the operational level the Soviet Air Force (Voyenno-Vozdushnye Silly, V-VS), was always subjected to the control of the local theatre command, nearly always run by army/ground-forces commanders. If there was anything common to the Cuban and Soviet military commanders, then it was that both expected air power to play no important role in the war in Angola. Moreover, because of the way the GenStab expected the Soviet armed forces to fight their next war, and because this branch was the sole procurement authority for the Soviet armed forces, the GenStab also dictated how all the aircraft were to be designed and equipped, what their performance was expected to be, and what kind of missions were they to fulfil. It also dictated how the Soviet armed forces were to be trained – which in turn influenced the way the Soviets trained their allies abroad. In Angola of the 1970s and the 1980s, this was to become the principal reason for a host of problems experienced with the deployment of air power – and the defence against it.

The Mess of 1976-1981

Considering such differences on the political and military level and a host of local problems caused by overoptimistic planning and incompetent and corrupt governance, it is unsurprising that a major rift developed between two wings of the MPLA's leadership. This led to the coup-attempt of May 1977, crushed with help of Cuban and loyal troops. This affair and the Cuban eagerness to downscale an involvement that was a growing burden for that nation's economy were two primary reasons for the FAR to decrease its troop presence in Angola to about 17,000 by 1978.

In turn, and especially following Neto's death in September 1979, the MPLA's leadership degenerated into a corrupt oligarchy, not even interested in countering the resurrected insurgency of UNITA. Indeed, the primary aim of the FAPLA remained defence from possible invasions from Zaire or South Africa, and the mass of its best trained and best equipped conventional units took no part in fighting the insurgency: they spent most of the II Angolan War deployed along a heavily fortified defence line stretching from Namibe on the Atlantic coast around over 300 kilometres (186 miles) to Menongue in central Angola – dubbed the Fidel Castro Line.

Meanwhile, in 1976, Luanda reinforced its campaign of supporting the insurgency of the South West Africa People's Organisation (SWAPO) in South-West Africa (SWA): in 1976,

Table 1: FAPA/DAA, FAPLA and FAR Terminology

Abbreviation	Native Name	Translation and Notes
BAT	Brigada de Artilharia Terrestre	Ground artillery Brigades
BDAA	Brigada de Defesa Anti-Aérea	Anti-Aircraft Missile Brigade
BFAA	Brigada de Foguete Anti-aérea	Anti-aircraft Rocket Brigade
BrDA	Brigada de Desembarque e Assalto	Disembarking and assault (airborne) brigade (FAPLA)
BrFE	Brigada de Forças Especiais	'special purpose' or special forces brigade, equivalent to Soviet Spetsnatz
BrI	Brigada de Infantaria	infantry brigade (FAPLA)
BrIM	Brigada de Infantaria Motorizada	motorized infantry brigade (FAPLA)
BrIN	Brigada de Intervenção	intervention brigade (FAPLA)
BrIL	Brigada de Infantaria Ligeira	light infantry brigade (FAPLA)
BT	Brigada de Tanques	tank brigade (FAR)
CIR	Centro de Instrução Revolucionária	revolutionary training centre (MMCA/FAPLA)
CORL	Companhia Rádio Localização	radio-location company (FAPA/DAA)
DEEM	Direcção de Estabelecimentos de Ensino Militares	Military Education Establishment (FAPLA)
ENAL	Escola Nacional de Aviação Ligeira	National Light Aviation School (FAPA/DAA)
ENAM	Escola Nacional de Aviação Militar	National Military Aviation School (FAPA/DAA)
GAAA	Grupo de Artiharia Anti-Aerea	anti-aircraft group (FAPA/DAA)
GT		tactical group (primary COIN unit of the FAPLA until 1978, but also a battalion-sized tactical group of every Cuban RIM in Angola)
LCB	Lucha contra Bandidos	official FAR term for COIN
ODP	Organização de Defesa Popular	People's Defence Organisation; MPLA/FAPLA-controlled militia
RAC	Regimento de Aviação de Caça	fighter aviation regiment (FAPA/DAA)
RACB	Regimento Aviação de Caça-Bombardeiro	fighter-bomber aviation regiment (FAPA/DAA)
RA/DAAN	Região Aérea de Defesa Anti-Aérea Norte	Northern Air Defence Region (FAPA/DAA)
RA/DAAS	Região Aérea de Defesa Anti-Aérea Sul	Southern Air Defence Region (FAPA/DAA)
RAH	Regimento Aéreo de Helicóptero	helicopter aviation regiment (FAPA/DAA)
RAL	Regimento de Lucha Contra Bandas Mercenarias	regiment for combat against mercenary bands (FAR)
RATM	Regimento Aéreo de Transporte Misto	mixed transport aviation regiment (FAPA/DAA)
RIM	Regimento de Infataria Motorizada	motorized infantry regiment (FAR)
RTRT	Regimento de Tropas Rádio Tecnicas	regiment of radio-technical troops (FAPA/DAA)

SWAPO re-located its headquarters from Zambia to Angola. Bolstered by an undisrupted influx of arms and volunteers, during the following years its organisation was vastly expanded, and its military wing – the People's Liberation Army of Namibia (PLAN) – began mounting ever larger infiltration attempts into SWA. As the number and intensity of PLAN's incursions continued to grow, South African Defence Forces (SADF) began to retaliate through 'externals': limited-scope offensives ever deeper into Angola, each aimed at the destruction of specific camps or complexes of bases belonging to SWAPO/PLAN.

The II Angolan War thus became a true 'War of Intervention' – as this conflict is now known in Angola. In addition to attacking SWAPO/PLAN in Angola, in attempt to dissuade or at least distract the MPLA, the South Africans also began supporting UNITA. In turn, SADF's externals and support for UNITA prompted the Cubans to make their 'return to Angola': in 1981-1983, they bolstered their troop presence to about 40,000 – primarily with the aim of increasing their COIN capabilities. Undeterred, but still unable to match the South African military superiority, Luanda

requested that SWAPO establish a conventional force and integrate it within the FAPLA, to help counter the South Africans and UNITA. At the same time, and because of the MPLA's preference for Soviet advice, Cuban COIN operations remained limited in duration and scope: for all practical purposes UNITA was left free to grow and advance ever further into Angola. Amid the decaying condition of the FAPLA, the importance of the MMCA Cubans grew once again: they not only had to undertake all of the major sweeps, operate the artillery and the air force, but also to keep all the major road communications free from the insurgency, to escort supply convoys, and to contribute ever more troops to the protection of critical infrastructure. The war thus went on, constantly growing in intensity: for Cuba, it began resembling what the Vietnam War was for the USA, while for Angola it required ever larger investment in the build-up of the FAPLA, which in turn gulped ever more of the always-meagre national resources, which were further damaged by continuous warfare.

2
People's Air Force

Standard English-language histories of the Angolan air force start with the independence of the country, on 11 November 1975: it is little known that what from 1975 until 1992 was officially termed the Angola People's Air Force and Anti-Aircraft Defence (*Força Aérea Popular de Angola/Defesa Anti-Aérea*, FAPA/DAA), was established in January 1976, or that by the time there was already a group of native and foreign pilots and ground crews operating a sizeable fleet of transport aircraft. It is even less well known that the origins of the FAPA/DAA reach back into the 1960s. Often, there is the impression that the Angolan air force did not exist before the mid-1980s, and played no significant role during in the war against multiple insurgencies and the South Africans during that decade; and that, if any actions were undertaken by Angolan aircraft, then they were flown by Cuban, Soviet, or even 'East German' advisors. While some of the early history of the FAPA/DAA, and early operations of the DAA/FAR in Angola have been covered in earlier volumes of this series, the following chapter is dedicated to an in-depth study of 1976-1979, in order to enhance the understanding of subsequent developments.

Portuguese origins

At 1,246,620 square kilometres, Angola is a huge country: the seventh largest in Africa, and the 23rd largest on Earth: roughly twice the size of France or Texas. Although inhabited since the Palaeolithic Era it was formed as a state only during the last few decades of the 400-years-long Portuguese colonisation: the Portuguese originally established only a few coastal settlements and trading posts in the 16th century, and began settling in the interior only in the 19th century. Present day borders came into being only during the early 20th century. Good land connections – like roads and railroads – were always few in number and thus air transportation rapidly grew in importance.

The first to fly an aircraft over Angola was the Portuguese Major Joaquim de Almeida Baltazar: in 1937, he was commissioned by the Ministry of the Colonies to bring an aircraft from the Belgian Congo to Luanda and establish the local aeroclub. Only a year later, on 8 September 1938, and together with another pilot, Fernando Albuquerque Bossa, Baltazar established a transport enterprise that eventually grew into the Air Transport Division of Angola (Divisão dos Transportes Aéros, DTA). The DTA launched its operations on 17 July 1940, flying one Klemm K1.31A-14 (registered as CR-LAS) and two de Havilland DH.89A Dragon Rapides (registered as CR-LAT and CR-LAV). In 1945, this fleet was reinforced through the acquisition of three Douglas DC-3s (including CR-LBK and CR-LBM), which remained in service until 1976. During the 1940s and 1950s, the requirement for air transportation grew to such an extent that not only was the original runway outside Luanda expanded, but by the 1950s civilian aerodromes with paved runways were constructed outside Soyo, Malanje, and Cafunfo in the north; Novoa Lisboa (Huambo), Silva Porto (Kuito), Luso (Luena) and Cangamba in central Angola; and Mocamedes (Namibe), Lubango, Menongue, and Cuito Cuanavale in the south. The bulk of the latter served the local and international businesses, which by 1974 operated over 100 light transport aircraft, most of which were privately owned. Meanwhile, the DTA initiated further expansion: in 1973, it was re-organised as the TAAG Aerial Transports of Angola (TAAG Transportes Aéros de Angola; colloquially 'TAAG'), and entered negotiations with Boeing for the acquisition of two Boeing 737 airliners and conversion training of 12 pilots in the USA, and for the installation of radar-supported air traffic control at all major airports in Angola, worth US$30 million.[1]

The reason for such a rapid growth of aviation in the Portuguese overseas province of Angola during the early 1970s was the discovery of oil and diamonds – which in turn attracted foreign businesses. From 1968, Gulf Oil from the USA began pumping 150,000 barrels a day from oilfields in the Cabinda Enclave, for which it was paying a royalty of US$500 million per year to the Portuguese authorities. Mobil Oil was to follow in fashion, while the South African De

The Portuguese left behind a number of well-constructed, even if small airports in Angola. This was the main terminal of Sa de Bandeira (Lubango) airport, seen after it was secured by UNITA in late 1975. Subsequently renamed Lubango, this facility became the centre of the early Angolan military aviation (and that of the Cuban military aviation's deployment in Angola). (Albert Grandolini Collection)

Beer Group began exploiting diamonds from the Soyo area.[2]

Although the history of military flying in Portugal dates back to the early 1910s, the Portuguese Air Force (Força Aérea Portuguesa, FAP) was officially established as a separate branch of the armed forces only in 1952 – about a year after the country joined NATO, and began receiving funding to enable it to deploy two operational squadrons of jet fighters (Republic F-84 Thunderjets) for use in the event of a war with the Soviet-dominated Warsaw Pact.[3] Under its highly flexible hierarchy, FAP units were deployed and re-deployed frequently, as available and necessary at a given point in time. Correspondingly, aerodromes, airfields, and air bases were spread over very

Another important airport constructed by the Portuguese was that of Nova Lisboa: renamed Huambo following independence, it became one of the most important facilities of this kind in central Angola – while many of the light civilian transports, like the Piper PA-23 Aztec visible in the foreground, were requisitioned by the nascent FAPA/DAA. (Albert Grandolini Collection)

different parts of the metropolitan and overseas territories, and units shifted from one place to another at short notice: during the 1960s it was a frequent occurrence that the same squadron would operate detachments deployed to three or four territories and twice as many bases over extended periods of time. Nevertheless, the home-bases of the FAP provided the basis for the entire designation and organisational system of the air force, and its nomenclature. On the top of this hierarchy was the Basa Aérea: a fully developed military air base (AB), with permanently based FAP units. The second most important type of installation was an Aeródromo Base: an airfield built for civilian purposes, but with secondary military purpose. Initially at least, the FAP invested next to nothing in Angola. This changed rapidly due to the growing tensions with local nationalists and then the outbreak of an insurgency. In October 1960, the construction of a major military airfield outside Luanda was initiated. Upon becoming operational, in May 1961, this was designated Aeródromo Base 9: following further expansion, its status was elevated to that of Basa Aérea 9, even if no permanently stationed units were deployed there for several years longer. In February 1961 the construction of a major airfield began outside Negage: this received the designation Aeródromo Base 3 and was followed by another such installation constructed outside Henrique de Carvalho (re-named Saurimo, post-independence), which became Aeródromo Base 4. Furthermore, the FAP began making use of a host of simpler and smaller airfields and aerodromes constructed for civilian purposes. They all received paved runways and were assigned military designations, becoming known as Manoeuvre Aerodromes (Aeródromo de Manobras, AMs). For example, AMs were constructed outside Maquela do Zombo (AM.31), Toto (AM.32), Portugália (AM.41), Camaxilo (AM.42), Cazombo (AM.43), and Cabinda (AM.95). Several transit airfields (Aeródromo de Transito, ATs) – essentially dirt strips – were also constructed, including those outside Cacolo, Santa Eulália, and Vial Teixeira de Sousa. Overall, by 1974, there were no fewer than 230

aerodromes around Angola: 25 of these had paved runways longer than 2,500 metres (8,202ft).[4]

This sprawling network supported the operations of the FAP's Operational Group 901: headquartered at Luanda AB, this included a mixed squadron of North American T-6G Texans, Auster Model D.5s, Dornier Do.27A/Os, and Douglas C-47 Dakotas, and – depending on availability and requirement – a squadron each of Lockheed P2Vs and Douglas B-26B/Cs; Douglas C-54s and Nord N.2502 Noratlas transports; Republic F-84G Thunderjet and then Fiat G.91R-4 jet fighter-bombers; and Aérospatiale SE.315B Alouette II, Aérospatiale SE.316B Alouette III, and Aérospatiale SA.330 Puma helicopters. During the final phase of the war, the F-84Gs were decommissioned without a substitute: plans to acquire Dassault Mirage III fighter-bombers never materialised and thus the FAP used old T-6Gs and slightly more recent B-26s for fire-support, while helicopters such as the Alouette III and Puma served as the mainstay of assault operations, and Dornier Do.27s, C-47s and Noratlases served at the forefront of transport operations. However, except for disused or non-operational examples, the mass of these were withdrawn by early 1975.

Pioneers

Immediately after the Carnation Revolution of 25 April 1974, the Portuguese armed forces suspended all of their combat activities against all nationalist movements in Angola. Indeed, their commanders were advised to permit the insurgents to come into the open: in October 1974, the Portuguese allowed the FNLA, MPLA and UNITA to establish an official presence in Luanda. Knowing of the MPLA's popularity in the Angolan capital, they entered close cooperation with that movement and agreed to establish a joint, 48,000-strong armed forces as the future military of Angola. However, as soon as the agreement – the Alvor Accord – became known, a mass exodus of the Portuguese colons began, followed by the general withdrawal of the Portuguese armed forces: by November 1975, over 300,000 civilians had left the country, mostly on board civilian airliners. With a few dozen exceptions, and at a single stroke, Angola lost nearly all of its experienced administrators and the whole skilled workforce. This withdrawal of the Portuguese population was due to the insecurity of the large cities and uncertainty regarding the future of the territory.

Before being officially permitted to enter Luanda, the MPLA's activity inside Angola always suffered from massive problems related to poor communications and lack of supplies. Precisely those problems were the reason for its leadership developing the idea of creating its own aviation arm in the mid-1960s. Correspondingly, two militants – João Felipe Neto 'Dimbõndwa' and Joaquim Portugal 'Chiloango' – were sent to the USSR for pilot-training and an attempt was launched to acquire Antonov An-2 biplane transports from a friendly country, which were to make supply flights to isolated insurgent bases around Angola.[5]

While this plan was never realised, related affairs became much easier once the MPLA entered open alliance with the Portuguese authorities: in late October 1974, ten combatants were assigned to the Portuguese instructor José Coutinho, and brought to Cabinda airfield to undergo pilot training. A month later, two other members of the MPLA were assigned to the Portuguese pilot Jaime José Rodrigues Pinto at Malanje, where they were trained in flying Auster D.5s. As far as is known, one of the latter group was the first Angolan ever to fly solo, in February 1975. By that time, Neto and the first commander of the FAPLA – and later also the first Minister of Defence of Angola – Henrique 'Iko' Carreira, tasked Commander José Manuel Paiva 'Bula Matadai' – freshly returned from an advanced officer course in the USSR – with studying the option of creating an Angolan air force.[6]

How far Bula Matadai developed any kind of design for an air force remains unclear. What is certain is that by February-March 1975 the first 350 members of the MMCA were in the country and nothing of their work was related to such an idea. Thus, it was only in August 1975 – once the MPLA had forced the FNLA and UNITA to withdraw from the Angolan capital – that the first group of Cuban aviation specialists began arriving, with the aim of helping the MPLA convert Luanda International Airport (IAP) into the main hub of its flying operations. Proceeded by Colonel Jaime Archer Silva and Lieutenant-Colonel Angel Botello Avila, this included people with extensive experience in operating US-made aircraft and helicopters, such as Francesco Pita Alonso, Jorge Quintana Barbosa, Hases Ramos Negrin, Alberto Ortega Segrera, René Corredera Brito,

Circo Vargas Guerra, Raúl Vigo Diaz, Aníbal Cofiño Bombino, and Ramón Herrera Morejón. Together with other members of the MMCA, and with the complicity of the Portuguese authorities, they secured Luanda IAP – enabling the MPLA and the Cubans to make full use of it – and then helped launch a recruiting drive amongst Angolans already undergoing pilot-training by Portuguese pilots, better-educated Luandans, and the Portuguese that were still around. The Portuguese known to have joined the FAPLA around this time include José M. Egrejas Borges Ervedosa (a retired Major of the FAP, who had served in Mozambique), Fernando José Pereira Jardim Ferreira and Júlio Cāndido da Cunha 'Cunha Maluco', and technicians António Magueira and José Carlos Sebastião. This was how the General Angolan Air Force (Força Aérea Geral Angolana) came into being.[7]

Starting from Scratch

The issue of finding suitable aircraft might have appeared easy at first glance, but was that was not to be the case. Certainly enough, the FAP and such companies as DAT, TAAG, and the Civilian Aeronautical Transport Service left behind dozens of aircraft in Angola. Military types including a total of 8 Douglas B-26 Invaders, 11 North American T-6 Texans, 4 C-47s, 4 Nord N.2501/2502 Noratlas, 2 Cessna 337s, 2 Grumman American AA-5s, and up to a dozen Dornier Do.27s littered Luanda IAP. However, except for two C-47s, two Cessnas, and two AA-5s, all of these were disused or had been non-operational since 1973; others had crucial assemblies removed and many were simply wrecked.[8] Civilian aircraft were in a much better condition and included four Douglas DC-3s (civilian variant of the C-47), and a miscellany of Auster D.5s, at least one each of Piper PA-23 Aztec, Piper PA-28 Cherokee and Piper PA-32 Cherokee 6, and various Cessna marks. Moreover, the Cubans found two Aérospatiale SE.315B Alouette II Lamas, and six Aérospatiale SE.316B Alouette III helicopters owned by the DIAMANG Corporation inside a hangar at Luanda IAP. All of these were promptly pressed into service, mainly to support MMCA and FAPLA activities around the country. However, none of the aircraft or helicopters was armed: it was only a few weeks later that the Cubans equipped one of the Alouette IIIs with the sight and launch rails for Soviet-made 9M14 Malyutka (ASCC/NATO-code 'AT-3 Sagger') anti-tank guided missiles (ATGMs). However, this experiment proved unsuccessful due to the lack of a stabilised sight

Despite countless reports of large numbers of combat aircraft left behind by the FAP and then pressed into service by the nascent Angolan air force, the mass of what the Portuguese left behind was useless wreckage. This photograph from 1976 shows two out of dozens of wrecks at Luanda IAP: the front one probably belonged to a Lockheed PV-2 and the rear to a B-26. (Albert Grandolini Collection)

WAR OF INTERVENTION IN ANGOLA VOLUME 3: ANGOLAN AND CUBAN AIR FORCES, 1975-1985

A closer look at the nose of one of the ex-FAP PV-2s abandoned at Luanda IAP reveals the insignia of Esquadron 91 and the openings for three machine guns installed under its nose. (Albert Grandolini Collection)

At least one Piper PA-28 Cherokee is known to have been operated by the Angolan air force. This photograph shows it with one of the pilots of 1975-1976 period (probably ex-Portuguese). It was the crew of one such light aircraft that experienced the first known air combat over Angola, fought in early November 1975. (Albert Grandolini Collection)

should have been recognised as unsubstantiated: the lack of such aircraft was the obvious reason for the MPLA's decision – almost certainly influenced by advisors of the MMCA – to place orders for Soviet-made MiG-17Fs and MiG-21MFs, around the same time.[10]

At this point in time, it was the governments of Congo-Brazzaville and Mozambique that provided crucial support by donating three ex-FAP Nord N.2501/2502 Noratlas transports and two additional ex-FAP C-47/DC-3s. These arrived together with two additional pilots – including José Calheiros Coutinho – and one aircraft was promptly used by Ervedosa to fly Soviet arms unloaded from ships at Pointe Noire to Luanda. Sometimes, Ervedosa was ordered to fly south and that was when things could become quite risky. The extent of this became obvious on 26 October 1975, when he arrived at the airport of Sá de Bandeira around the same time that it was being secured by South African troops. Ervedosa turned the aircraft around and barely managed to climb again to return safely to Mocamedes.[11] According to Russian sources, during the following days the ex-Mozambiquan Noratlases transferred a battery of BM-21 multiple rocket launchers (MRLs) from Maputo to Luanda: in turn, these played a crucial role in defeating the combined FNLA-Zairian offensive at Quifangondo, on 10 November 1975. All available sources leave no doubt that all the available pilots – Cuban, Portuguese or Mozambiquan – were flying 'excessive numbers of flight hours' in support of the MMCA and FAPLA around this time.[12]

for guiding the missile, and was abandoned: it was only in 1981 that the Angolans began installing Soviet-made UB-16-57 pods for 57mm S-5 unguided rockets on their Alouettes again, even if the practical results of such experiments were once again poor. Meanwhile, by 20 October 1975, 35 Angolan cadets were assembled at Luanda IAP: they were then flown to Cabinda to undergo a pilot-training course with the help of light aircraft.[9]

With hindsight, it can be concluded that all the rumours about the FAP leaving behind Fiat G.91R-4 fighter-bombers, circulated in the Western press for most of the 1970s, 1980s, and the 1990s,

Table 2: ex-Portuguese Nord N.2501/2502 Noratlas Transports in Angola[13]		
Type	ex-FAP Serial	Angolan /registration
N.2502F	6407	D2-EPD
N.2502B	6415	D2-EPS

N.2501D	6424	D-2EPT
N.2502A	6405	D2-EPV
N.2501D	6425	D2-EPY
N.2501A	6401	D2-E??
N.2502B	6413	D2-E??
N.2501D	6416	D2-E??

Mercenary Air Raid

The MPLA was not the only Angolan nationalist movement in the process of creating an air force: on behalf of the FNLA, the CIA was meanwhile taking steps in a similar direction. To support its foreign mercenaries and Holden Roberto's advance on Luanda, the Americans organised an air bridge from the USA and Europe to Zaire, including Lockheed C-130 Hercules and Lockheed C-141B StarLifters of the US Air Force, and then from Kinshasa to airfields in western Zaire, including Lockheed L-100 Hercules transports operated by the CIA's front companies. Moreover, by August 1975, the FNLA was supported by a small air wing including one Piper Aztec; several Beechcraft B.55 Barons; one each Cessna 172, Cessna 180, and Cessna 310; one Rockwell TurboCommander, three Fokker F.27s and one Alouette II helicopter. Additional aircraft from South Africa, Rhodesia and Zaire were chartered as necessary. While the entire effort proved rather 'too little, too late', sensing an emergency, the Americans attempted to speed up the air bridge from Kinshasa to various airfields in northern Angola.[14]

This is how it came to be that one of the FNLA-supporting Barons, operated by a group of Portuguese mercenaries, was deployed to Ambriz, about 160 kilometres (99.4 miles) north of Luanda. Before long, the mercenaries detected the activity of transports and light aircraft underway in support of the FAPLA garrison of the Margarida ranch, in Sumbe, about 300 kilometres (186.4 miles) from the Angolan capital, and decided to try shooting down one of these. For this purpose, they installed a 7.62mm Browning M1919 machine gun firing through a side window of the Baron, and then waited for their opportunity. At an unknown date in early November 1975, the Portuguese managed to intercept a Cherokee 6 hauling supplies for the FAPLA and hit it with several bullets. Nevertheless, the FAPLA crew managed to return safely to Luanda. Elated, the mercenaries then planned to raid the main transmitter of the Luanda Radio Club. For this purpose, they used a Cessna 180 carrying two bags of plastic explosives, weighting about 50kg (110lbs) each. This air raid was flown on 8 November 1975, and proved highly successful: although both sacks were dropped manually out of the side doors, they hit the antennas, knocking them out.[15] Certainly enough, the MPLA – with the help of Cuban technicians – managed to repair the facility, but the strike made Neto and other leaders in Luanda uneasy, and prompted them to order a significant reinforcement of air defences around the Angolan capital.

Aircraft operated by the mercenaries recruited by the CIA on behalf of the FNLA continued their operations during the following weeks: indeed, three of them were widely reported as being deployed as makeshift bombers that attacked the FAPLA positions early during the battle of Quifangondo on 10 November 1975. Actually, the jets in question were English Electric Canberras of the South African Air Force which crossed Botswana underway to Angola and then operated at high altitude to undertake an 'area-bombing' mission (instead of all targeting a specific aiming point), in order to avoid being clearly identified. Most of their bombs missed their targets widely, in turn provoking no retaliation from a group of Guinean air defence specialists commanded by Sanussi

One of the Cuban pilots that joined the nascent General Angolan Air Force in October-November 1975 (or one of the Portuguese that followed in fashion a few months later), proudly posing in front of a requisitioned Piper PA-23 Aztec, already camouflaged in dark green overall (see colour section for details). (Albert Grandolini Collection)

Soares Cassamá and equipped with Soviet-made 9K92M Strela-1M (ASCC/NATO-codename 'SA-7b Grail') man-portable air defence systems (MANPADs) for the protection of the FAPLA.[16]

Cuban Military Intervention

Once Angola was officially released into independence, on 11 November 1975, there was no reason any more for Havana to hold back. Correspondingly, when launching Operation Carlota, they decided to deploy a sizeable contingent of DAA/FAR pilots and ground crews to Angola. Additional Cuban pilots were thus in action very soon – and they flew not only transports but also light aircraft, some of which were frequently used for reconnaissance purposes. It was during one such mission that on 25 December 1975 the Cessna 310 flown by Major Juan Céspedes was hit by fire from a South African operated 20mm anti-aircraft gun while underway from Mussende to Cariango. The pilot survived and managed a safe landing. However, his passenger, Major Edilberto Fonseca of Cuban military intelligence, was killed.[17]

A day later, at least five giant Antonov An-22 transport aircraft of the Soviet Air Force's Military Transport Aviation (Voyenno-Transportnaya Aviatsiya, VTA) arrived at Luanda IAP to unload nine MiG-17F jet fighter-bombers and one MiG-15UTI. On the same day, the DAA/FAR selected a group of versed fighter-bomber pilots for deployment to Angola. Led by Rafael del Pino, who was already in Luanda, this group included José A Montes (commander of the future MiG-17-unit), Eusebio Carmenate Pedroso, Armando González Nodarse, Felipe González Reyes, Darío Domínguez Melgarejo, Celso Avial Rodríguez, Pedro Luis Casbella Martinez, and Rolando Santiesteban. After undergoing an intensive air combat course, they were flown to Luanda on board an Ilyushin Il-62M transport of the Soviet airline Aeroflot on 7 January 1976. The build-up of the MiG-17 unit in Angola was delayed when most of the Soviet personnel tasked with assembling and flight-testing the MiGs poisoned themselves by drinking pure alcohol during the evening of 6 to 7 January: Moscow then dispatched a new team, and the first three MiG-17s and the sole MiG-15UTI were assembled and declared ready for operations on 19 January 1976.[18]

Communists to the Rescue

Meanwhile, at an unknown date in January 1976, seven former officers of the Portuguese armed forces – all members of the

Rafael del Pino making a low-altitude, high-speed pass at Luanda International in the MiG-17F serial number C22. Visible in the background are a miscellany of wrecked PV-2s, B-26s, Do.27s, and Noratlas transports left behind by the FAP. (via Luis Dominguez)

Communist Party – arrived in Luanda to request political asylum. Among them were four former G.91R-4 pilots, including (Colonel) José Costa Martins – who had been minister in the provisional government of Vasco Gonçalves in Lisbon – João Pimentel, João Jorge Mirenda, and Martins Jorge, and three other pilots, Frederico Lopes, Barreto Ferreira 'Xixas', and Maximiliano Caroco. All had taken part in a failed communist-instigated coup attempt in Lisbon of 25 November 1975. All were well-accepted by the MPLA, and – desperate to provide the FAPLA troops with close-air-support – Ike Carreira promptly provided them with commendation letters, before forwarding them straight to Rafael del Pino: on finding the Cuban commander, they explained to him that they had been sent by the Communist Party of Portugal to help out. Rather startled, but also constrained by Fidel Castro's personal order banning any kind of combat operations by his MiGs, the Cuban was left without a choice but to return them to Carreira. Eventually, all the seven Portuguese officers were integrated into the FAPLA and flew C-47/DC-3s and Noratlas transports.[19]

Establishment of the FAPA

The intensive activity of helicopters and transport aircraft, and then the MiGs flying over Luanda could not escape public attention and thus on 21 January 1976, Agostinho Neto – now acting as the first president of independent Angola – rushed to officially announce the establishment of the FAPA at Luanda IAP. During a big ceremony celebrating this occasion, Neto defined the tasks of the new branch as defence of national airspace against foreign violations and external aggression, support of ground forces on Angolan territory, and support of the economic reconstruction of the country, and appointed Comandante (Major) João Filipe Neto 'Dimbõndwa' as its first commander (with Comandante Xisto Bandeira as Chief-of-

Staff). This might appear as a big masquerade at first glance, because – at least according to the Cubans – Dimbondwa had nothing to say in the presence of highly-experienced Cuban officers.[20] However, more recent Angolan accounts reveal a different picture: therefore, the FAPA originally consisted of three flying units, based in Luanda, Saurimo and Negage, as listed in Table 3 but excluded the Cuban-manned contingent. Indeed, even if wearing Angolan insignia (though no Angolan national flags), and demonstratively presented as 'Angolan' to the domestic and international press during the establishment-ceremony at Luanda IAP on 21 January 1976, the MiG-17 unit was not only entirely staffed by Cubans, but also outside FAPA's chain of command. This was valid for the next two units to come into being after, on 23 January 1976, VTA's An-22s unloaded the first two out of a total of 12 MiG-21MF interceptors at Luanda IAP – and the equipment for a battery of S-125 Pechora (ASCC/NATO-codename 'SA-3 Goa') surface-to-air missiles (SAMs). Once again, both were entirely staffed by DAA/FAR personnel. Within the first group of Cuban MiG-21 pilots deployed in Angola were Emer Juan Pita, Benigno González Cortés, Huberto Trujillo Hernández, Alejandro Morejón Gálvez, Albio Córdova Monterón, Antonio Rojas Marrero, Roberto Canar Alvarez, Pedro L. Colmero Lauredo, Evelio Bravo Martin, Fidel Vargas Rabelo, Argelio Cardes Reyes, and Eduardo González Sarría. The latter, then a youngster keen to fly brand-new MiG-21MFs in combat – especially after an SAAF Canberra overflew Luanda IAP on a reconnaissance sortie – recalled: 'The organisation was such that our operational commander was receiving orders from the commander of the MMCA, which meant we were subjected to the army. We had very strict rules of engagement, including a strict prohibition of attacks on the South Africans… Our MiG-21s received serials from C40 to C51.'[21]

For support of the two combat squadrons, a single Ilyushin Il-18 transport of the Cubana de Aviacion airline was forward deployed at Luanda: stripped of its seats, it was used to make regular transport flights to Saurimo and Luso, and – once this town was recovered from UNITA (see below for details) – to Huambo. Finally, in May 1976, the Soviets delivered four Mil Mi-8 assault helicopters, which were also crewed by the Cubans.[22]

In other words: although not obvious to the outside world, as of early 1976 'two' Angolan air forces came into being: one, operating the mass of transports and light aircraft, staffed by Angolan and Portuguese personnel, and commanded by Dimbõndwa; and another, operating what were actually Angolan-owned MiGs, Alouette II/III and Mi-8 helicopters, staffed by the Cubans, commanded by del Pino.

Table 3: FAPA, February 1976[23]		
Unit	**Equipment**	**Notes**
Esquadra de Transportes	2 C-47/DC-3, 7 N.2501/2502	CO 2nd Lieutenant António Guilherne Hernab Gonçalves Mangueira 'Nunucha'
Esquadra de Reconhecimento	2 AA-5, 1 B.55, 2 PA-23, 1 Shrike Commander	CO 1st Lieutenant Kanga José
Esquadrilha de Cessna	Reims-Cessna FR-172-K, 2 Cessna 337	CO unknown; unit tasked with training and reconnaissance, and also light attack

A MiG-17F covered with a tarpaulin seen parked at the edge of the runway of Luanda International in January 1976. At the time, the media was abuzz with reports about 'thousands of Cuban troops, supported by tanks' arriving to support the MPLA. Therefore, the new government in Luanda was left with little choice but to officially announce the establishment of an Angolan air force. (Tom Cooper Collection)

A group of young officers and other ranks of the nascent FAPA, presenting arms during the establishment ceremony on 21 January 1976. Visible in the background are (from left to right), a Noratlas and a C-47 Dakota transport, the Tupolev Tu-135 airliner (used as a VIP-transport), and one of the first six SE.316B Alouette helicopters of the Angolan air force. (Albert Grandolini Collection)

Colonel João Filipe Neto 'Dimbõndwa' (in uniform and field cap), seen leading Colonel Henrique Teles Carreira 'Iko' (foreground left, in light shirt) on a tour along the tarmac of Luanda IAP, together with a group of other Angolan officers, and at least one Cuban officer, in 1976. After serving as the first Minister of Defence of Angola, from 1975 until 1983, Iko took over as the commander of the FAPA/DAA in 1983. (Albert Grandolini Collection)

Castro's Micro-Management

While one might expect the Cuban-flown MiGs to soon be deployed in action against the FNLA in northern Angola, and UNITA and South African forces in central and southern Angola – no such thing happened. As mentioned above, Fidel Castro prohibited any kind of combat operations, except for the defence of Luanda. Considering that the Cuban leader advised officers of his units sent to Angola that the MPLA had no armed forces of their own, and that they would have to do all the fighting on their own, it appears that the motivation for this decision was his understanding of the critical vulnerability of not only the government in Luanda, but also the MMCA. The Cubans were deployed over 11,000 kilometres (roughly 6,800 miles) away from home and kept operational with the help of a resupply effort that required the mobilisation of almost all the airborne and seaborne transport assets of Cuba. Even if the Soviets had launched their air bridge to Luanda, in December 1975, followed by merchant ships, and although the number of FAR troops deployed in Angola increased to about 11,000 by the end of January 1976, for all practical purposes, the strategic position of the MMCA was precarious – if not critical – for several months. Therefore, throughout the period of November 1975 – January 1976, it was solely light aircraft of the FAPA's Esquadra de Reconhecimento, and Cuban-operated Alouette helicopters that were active over the battlefields in northern and central Angola. Certainly enough, their pilots flew hundreds of highly important reconnaissance missions, and frequently served as artillery spotters. Moreover, the sole AT-3-armed Alouette III flew several attacks on South African ground forces in the Ebo area from mid-November 1975. However, all South African reports of air strikes by 'MiG-17s' – some of which were dated in late December 1975 – were unsubstantiated. At most, they might be related to the activity of Soko J-21 Jastreb and G-2A Galeb light strikers operated by the Zambian Air Force, details about which remain elusive even at the time of writing.[24]

Castro proved ready to lift this ban only once it became obvious that the US, French and Zairian supported FNLA was beaten and de-facto fleeing from northern Angola on 1 February 1976. On this date, he granted permission for several light aircraft and helicopters to be re-deployed to the airport of M'banza-Kongo. Unintentionally, this led to the next known 'air combat' of this campaign. On 7 February 1976, an Alouette III flown by the Cuban pilot known only as 'Fedor' and tasked with reconnaissance of the road from Quibocolo to Saurimo, encountered a CIA-operated Cessna underway on a mission to support the FNLA. Neither the Alouette nor the Cessna were armed, but their crews carried multiple firearms with them, and began shooting at each other through the open windows of their aircraft. Fortunately for everybody involved, all the bullets missed.[25]

Mishap at Cela

Unsurprisingly considering the general chaos in a country more than half of which was still under foreign forces or the control of foreign-supported insurgents, and exaggerated reports about clashes with the FNLA in the north, the lack of coordination between the top commanders of the MMCA spoiled the next attempt of Rafael del Pino and his pilots to go into action. Once it became known that the South Africans had initiated their general withdrawal from central and southern Angola, the daunting Cuban decided to re-deploy his jets to the airport of Cela – which had the only sufficiently long (2,000m/6,600ft) metalled runway necessary to support operations by MiGs in that part of the country. However, the South Africans had sabotaged the runway on their withdrawal by cratering it in dozens of places. Lacking equipment and troops for repair works, the Cubans collected whatever cattle they could find at nearby farms abandoned by the Portuguese and offered these to the locals in exchange for their services. In response to the offer over 2,000 civilians gathered at the airport on the morning of 28 January 1976. Although using the most primitive methods imaginable, guided by the Cuban military engineer Echabasal, they helped repair the runway. The ground equipment – including fuel trucks, vehicles carrying auxiliary power units and other equipment necessary to operate combat aircraft – followed in a large convoy which arrived safely on 2 February. Because the Soviets flatly refused to deliver

more than one vehicle with compressed air for the brake system of the Angolan MiGs, the Cubans were forced to improvise: they loaded a stock of compressed-air bottles onto one of the vehicles, and then a similar stock of high-pressure tyres for their MiGs into another. However, as soon as this convoy reached the airport of Cela, and on order from Deputy Commander MMCA, General Rochelio Asevedo, it was re-routed to Negage – more than 800 kilometres (497 miles) away! As so many other 'army' officers, Asevedo was ignorant of necessities related to operating modern combat aircraft and was thus astonished at 'all the advanced equipment' deployed at Cela. Without asking any questions, he thus destroyed the planning and work of dozens of officers and technicians in a matter of minutes. It is almost unnecessary to add that it took the officers of the DAA/FAR contingent days to recover at least some of the equipment in question and even longer to bring it back to working order. Of course, the MiGs thus remained at Luanda IAP.[26]

Del Pino's Adventure

Through early February 1976, the strategic balance in Angola shifted in favour of the MPLA. Indeed, the South African withdrawal left UNITA in a vulnerable position. Wasting no time, the contemporary commander of the MMCA, General Abelardo Colomé Ibarra and his staff decided to deploy the combined Angolan-Cuban forces in a series of counteroffensives. In preparation for these, a 16-man-strong team of Cuban special forces led by Lieutenant Artemio Rodriguez Cuza was deployed by Alouette III helicopters 55 kilometres south of the Queve River on 2 February 1976. A few days later, the unit was detected by UNITA and surrounded. On 8 February, while visiting the HQ of the FAR's Southern Front Command, del Pino learned of this emergency: entirely on his own, and despite Castro's standing order not to operate jet fighters over that part of Angola, he decided to organise a rescue operation. On 9 February 1976, del Pino flew a single MiG-21MF armed with two UB-16-57 pods all the way from Luanda IAP to provide top cover for a pair of Alouette IIIs. Because of fierce ground fire, the helicopters could not land and pick up the troops. Operating in a great hurry because he was critically short on fuel, del Pino delivered just one attack, first unleashing all 32 of his rockets, and then spending all the ammunition from his internal 23mm cannon. With the opposition scattered in all directions, this time helicopter-crews experienced no problems with extracting the Cuban special forces. The Cuban pilot returned to Luanda on only a memory of fuel in his MiG-21MF's tanks.[27] Moreover, Del Pino found himself facing fierce critique from his superiors, as recalled by González Sarría: 'Combat operations were still strictly prohibited.

MiG-21MF C49 of the FAPA/DAA (piloted by a Cuban), rolling down the tarmac of Luanda IAP against the backdrop of local hangars. Visible in the background are three ex-FAP C-47s and a civilian-operated Fokker F.27. The MiG is loaded with three 400-litre drop tanks and rails for R-3S air-to-air missiles. (via Luis Dominguez)

Rafael del Pino violated that order and was almost stripped off his wings by the chief of the MMCA, and put under a house arrest until further notice'.

Eventually, the dauntless Cuban flier was saved from being demoted and subjected to a military court martial through personal intervention of Raul Castro, who stressed his earlier merits. Nevertheless, henceforth there were no end of reports about 'MiG strikes' from other parts of Angola. For example, on 10 February 1976, FAPLA troops reported a jet fighter high in the sky over Luena, and – later during the afternoon – 'MiG strikes' on UNITA positions in the town too. Whether these were propaganda-motivated claims or Zambian jets, remains unclear: available Cuban sources deny having flown any kind of combat sorties before mid-February.[28]

A Cuban-flown MiG-21MF returning from a combat sortie in northern Angola in 1976. Notable are empty hardpoints, indicating the release of all ordnance, which probably consisted of four FAB-250M-62 bombs. As far as is known, MiG-21MFs in Angola were only ever flown by Cuban pilots. (via Luis Dominguez).

Fishbeds over Huambo

Probably as a result of the del Pino affair, on 18 February 1975 Castro did grant permission for DAA/FAR-operated fighter jets to go into action, and a pair of MiG-21MFs flown by Humberto Trujillo and Alexandro Morchon were forward deployed to the airport of Huambo a day later. To avoid any kind of possible misunderstandings with MMCA, FAR, and FAPLA commanders, this time all the ground crews and support equipment were re-deployed on board a FAPA C-47, and a VTA Antonov An-12. By the end of the month, the rest of the Cuban 'MiG-21 Squadron' followed, and on 20, 21, and 26 February Trujillo flew a series of visual-reconnaissance sorties along the Benguela Railway.[29] Deliveries of additional equipment – mainly drop tanks – and fuel enabled 26 further reconnaissance sorties over southern Angola, sometimes all the way to the border with South West Africa. Meanwhile, the unit was 'reinforced' through the addition of a Cessna Skymaster, requisitioned from the Cuca Brewery: this aircraft was deployed as a 'squadron hack' – for liaison, but sometimes also for reconnaissance purposes. González Sarría recalled the type of sorties flown by him and his comrades from Huambo in March 1976 as follows:

We mostly escorted truck convoys, but also flew visual reconnaissance (carrying three drop tanks), combat air patrols (carrying four R-3S air-to-air missiles) and so on. Our armament consisted of up to four UB-16-57 rocket pods, each for 16 57mm rockets. Alternatively, our aircraft could carry two 500kg bombs, if operating from air bases on the sea level, or less heavier ones when operating from 'hot and high' runways, like in Huambo. Another weapon we deployed in Angola were S-24 240mm rockets. That was a very tricky weapon able to flame out the engine when fired.'

Hunt for Savimbi

On 8 March 1976, the MMCA ordered the re-deployment of four MiG-21MFs (flown by Benigno González Cortes, Emer Juan Bita, Alvio Cordova Mantecon, and Arhelio Cordero Rayes) to the airport of Luena in eastern central Angola. Ground crews and support equipment were transported by one of FAPA's Noratlases, while the fighter-bombers were supported by a single Alouette III (flown by Ases Ramos), and a Beech-18 (flown by del Pino). Once in Luena, the Cubans were informed about Savimbi planning to meet his top commanders in a church about one kilometre from the airport of Lumbala. They promptly set up an air strike – code-named Operation New Shoes. Originally planned for the morning of 9 March, this was spoiled by two factors. The Beech-18 – this time flown by Modesto Conception Puna – which was to establish the precise position of the church and then guide MiG-pilots into attack, was forced into a hurried withdrawal by several SA-7s fired at it. Subsequently, the target zone was subjected to torrential rain, which lasted for four days. Correspondingly, a new attempt was initiated on 13 March. This time, the Beech-18 was late in reaching the target zone due to massive clouds. Thus, the first pair of MiG-21MFs – flown by del Pino and Cortes, and armed with two S-24 240mm heavy unguided rockets each – descended out of the overcast about 2,000 metres (6,561ft) above Luena, only to find a Fokker F.27 transport of Air Zaire (registration 9Q-CLO) parked at the local airport and in the process of unloading food supplies from Rhodesia. Forgetting about his original target, del Pino dived to attack, exploiting the fact that his supersonic MiG could not be heard by those on the ground before it was too late. He unleashed both of his S-24s at the Fokker, followed by Cortes: their rockets not only obliterated the F.27, but also ruined the main terminal of the airport. The next two MiG-21MFs – flown by Bita and Cordoba – then bombed the runway and the main terminal. Between two and six SA-7s fired by FALA troops in return all missed the rapidly distancing fighter-bombers.[30]

The MiGs were hardly away when the belated Beech-18 finally appeared over Luena. After its crew found out that the actual target remained untouched, it observed another F.27 in the process of landing at the local airport. The pilot of the Beech called for the MiG-pilots to return and shoot the transport down, but they responded that they were out of ammunition and on the way back to Luena. Therefore, the flight mechanic positioned his 7.62mm RPK machine gun in the open door while the pilot steered in the direction of the approaching Fokker. However, the mercenary pilot recognised the approaching threat, pushed the throttles and accelerated away. Two hours later, the four MiG-21MFs returned to crater the runway at Lumbala with four FAB-250 bombs and hit the position of a UNITA mortar platoon near the Lufute River north of the airfield with four additional S-24s. The third attack on the airport of Lumbala took place on the morning of 14 March: better coordinated with the Beech-18 than before, two of the Cubans then cratered the runway with four additional 250kg bombs, while the other two plastered a nearby camp with a total of 128 57mm S-5 rockets. Heavy rain precluded further attacks – enabling UNITA's leader, Jonas Savimbi to escape the wrath of the Cuban MiG pilots – until del Pino decided to take off regardless of the weather, this time flying MiG-21MF serial C41, armed with two UB-32-57 rocket pods. Once airborne, he lost direction in the massive clouds, and eventually ran out of fuel before making an emergency landing on an airstrip outside Munhango, only recently secured by a company of FAPLA. Protected by Cuban troops flown in by two Alouettes, del Pino's MiG was refuelled and flown out by Humberto Trujillo with the help of SPRD-99 rocket-boosters brought in from Cuba for this purpose, on 23 March. However, visibly shaken by his experiences in Angola, del Pino was subsequently taken off flying fast jets: he was never to fly combat sorties again. Thus ended Operation New Shoes, in the course of which the Cuban 'MiG-21 Squadron' flew a total of 13 combat sorties, dropped 12 FAB-250 bombs, and fired 8 S-24 and 192 S-5 rockets, to destroy a single F.27, ruin the airport of Gago-Coutinho, and cause up to 100 casualties to the FALA.[31]

Destroying UNITA

The assault on UNITA in central and southern Angola went on through March 1976, with the combined MMCA-FAPLA units delivering one blow after the other. Subjected to a series of air strikes and ground advances, and while surviving the fall of Huambo, Savimbi lost scores of combatants killed or captured while withdrawing to Gago Coutinho (Lumbala), and then further south-east, between 8 February and 14 March. Menongue was secured by the MMCA and FAPLA in early April and a pair each of MiG-21MFs and MiG-17Fs promptly deployed there. Keen to kill or capture the insurgent leader, Cuban military intelligence was carefully monitoring his activities with the help of signals intelligence (SIGINT), and on 7 April 1976 it triangulated his radio traffic to the former Portuguese army base in Tempué. The place was subjected to air strikes from two MiG-21MFs (flown by Umerto Trujillo and Jaime Archer Silva) and four MiG-17Fs (led by Felipe González) forward deployed at Menongue. Altogether, the six MiGs expended a total of 128 S-5K rockets and 880 23mm shells, and 147 of 37mm calibre. On the same day, MiG-21MFs also struck Cangombe and Muie, and on 8 April four MiG-17Fs demolished a jetty on the Cuito Cuanavale River near the town of Vila Nova de Armada, and two camps outside the town of Cuito Cuanavale. UNITA attempted to hit back by raiding Menongue airport during the night from 11 to 12 April: they missed their target but prompted the Cubans to temporarily evacuate their MiGs to Mocamedes. Nevertheless, the Cubans returned a few days later, to launch additional air strikes. Finally, on 21 May 1976, MiG-21s narrowly missed Savimbi while heavily bombing Samasseca.[32]

The hunt for Savimbi was further reinforced once the Soviets delivered the first batch of 11 Antonov An-26 transports: while the first six were assigned to the FAPA's Escuadrón de Transportes, the other 5 – one of which (registered as T-50) was used as a VIP-transport by the MMCA – were taken up by the DAA/FAR-

contingent, and regularly deployed as bombers, as were two Angolan-operated examples. The Soviets then added another An-26 – equipped for transport of VIPs, and one An-30: both of these wore Aeroflot markings, and the latter (wearing the registration CCCP-11765) was used for reconnaissance and mapping purposes (with the help of aerial photography).[33]

Under immense pressure, between 21 June and 13 July 1976, the insurgent leader was forced to scatter his remaining forces to evade Cuban troops that were leap-frogging with the help of An-26s and Mi-8 helicopters. The immense size of UNITA's losses of this period show the fact that while starting this campaign with several thousands of insurgents trained by the South Africans, on 28 August 1976 Savimbi reached Cueilei accompanied by just 76 men.[34] The hunt for Savimbi was continued by the FAPA even once the ground forces stopped their advance into south-eastern Angola. Even Cessna 172s, Britten-Norman BN-2 Islanders, Alouette IIIs, and then An-26s of the FAPA began flying air strikes on any UNITA camp they could find, the lighter aircraft and helicopters using bombs made from beer bottles.[35]

Meanwhile, with a squadron each of MiG-17Fs and MiG-21s, and a half-squadron each of Mi-8s and An-26s deployed in Angola, the DAA/FAR formalised the status of these units in form of an 'Air Group', commanded by Enrique Carreras, with Raúl P James as deputy commander. One of the first tasks of the ground crews of the Air Group was to expand Cabinda airport and make it suitable for MiG-17 operations: as the centre of the Angolan oil industry, the area was the heart of the economy and thus of crucial importance for Luanda. Indeed, José A Montes' unit flew its first combat operations against the FLEC on 1 May 1976. Reinforced by Mi-8s, the unit then took part in operations that drove the surviving insurgents over the border into Zaire.[36]

Although heavily involved on three frontlines simultaneously, the MMCA and FAPLA still found enough resources to launch a drive against remaining groups of the FNLA in northern Angola. Cuban pilots were around to provide support. For example, operating from Negage airport, four MiG-21MFs, two MiG-17Fs and two An-26s bombed Massango and Mangando on 13 May, badly shaking the insurgents and forcing them to flee: indeed, by the end of the month, a combination of additional air strikes and ground advances smashed the insurgency: whoever could found refuge in Zaire. The near-simultaneous campaigns against the FLEC and the FNLA in the north and UNITA in the east and south of the spring and summer 1976 thus ended with an overwhelming success. The FLEC and the FNLA were smashed and forced to withdraw into Zaire, to a degree where neither would try re-entering Angola for years after. UNITA was virtually destroyed, and Havana was able to agree a cease-fire with Pretoria: the MPLA was thus in firm control of more than 90% of Angola.

3

Which Way Next?

If the campaign of 1976 secured nearly all of Angola for the MPLA, it was all but useless for that party's control of the economic development of the country. As described in the Volume 2 of this mini-series, Neto's government, genuinely interested in improving the living conditions of the Angolan population, launched all-encompassing education and welfare campaigns. Following early success, both proved overambitious and an ultimate failure. The reason was a combination of factors like a rapid decline in oil prices and other raw commodities exported by Angola, but also widespread incompetence and mismanagement, corruption, and growing spending for defence. Moreover, as Castro's analysis in written communication to the government in Luanda was to show, later on, and on Soviet advice, the MPLA's government spent all of the second half of the 1970s building-up a massive conventional force to defend the country against perceived threats from Zaire and South Africa: indeed, the FAPLA went through a period of uncontrolled growth. At the same time, the irregular threat was entirely ignored, and the issue of fighting the remaining insurgents was left to the MMCA – although Havana was eager to downsize its involvement to a bare minimum.[1]

Training, Training – and more Training

As the frontlines moved ever further away from Luanda through March, April, May and June 1976, the demand for support by transport aviation continued to grow. The FAPA's Esquadron de Transportes was meanwhile equipped with a total of two An-2s, six An-26s, two C-47/DC-3s, and seven Noratlases, but still heavily tasked.[2] Indeed,

sheer exhaustion led to its first confirmed loss, at an unknown date in 1976, when pilot Lourenco Manuel Gomes Neto 'Loló' made a hard landing with a Noratlas at the Cuangar airstrip in southern Angola. The aircraft that used to wear the FAP serial 6416 at earlier times – and FAPA registration T-40 since November 1975 – suffered such structural damage that it had to be written off.[3]

Unsurprisingly, on 28 March 1976, the FAPA hurriedly graduated 35 cadets undergoing training at Cabinda since October the previous year and promptly had them re-assigned. Nine were assigned as pilots to the Esquadron de Transportes (four as Alouette III pilots, converted to the type with help of a Portuguese pilot named Pedro, and an anonymous mechanic, and two to An-2s – delivered from the USSR in April 1976, together with a group of Soviet instructors). The remaining 26 graduates, and 75 new cadets were then sent for further training in the USSR. Over the following three years, eight of them (subsequently reinforced with a group of 20 future technicians) were qualified to fly Antonov An-2s; two to fly Antonov An-26s; while others were trained to fly Mi-8s and MiG-17s. About a dozen additional Angolan cadets were sent to the USSR in 1977: all for training on transport types, such as the An-2 and Yakovlev Yak-40. Once this group was back, in 1981, it was converted to An-26s in Angola.[4]

Table 4: FAPA, October 1978[6]		
Unit	Equipment	Notes
Esquadra de Transportes	7 N.2501/2502, 3 An-26, 2 C-47/DC-3, 2 An-2	3 N.2501 operational, 2 undergoing overhauls in Portugal
Esquadra de Reconhecimento e Ligação	2 Cessna 337, 1 Shrike Commander,	All aircraft non-operational
Esquadra de Helicópteros	2 Alouette II, 6 Alouette III	All operational

An FAPA/DAA An-26, seen in the early 1990s. A total of 22 were acquired by the Angolan air force between 1976 and 1987: while some were operated in civilian livery, and even more with civilian markings – as visible on the example here (registration D2-END) – all saw extensive service in support of the FAPLA, and about half a dozen even regularly flew air strikes armed with FAB-250M-62 and FAB-500M-62 general purpose bombs. (Tom Cooper Collection)

The TAAG airline followed in fashion: in late 1976, it pushed through its acquisition of two Boeing 737s and conversion training of two crews in the USA: even these airliners were occasionally used for transport of FAPLA troops. In 1978, the TAAG then sent six cadets for a training course on Yak-40s in the USSR, and another group for training on the same type at the Aviation Academy of the Yugoslav Air Transport in Vršac. Both groups were back in the country by 9 September 1979, by when the TAAG had opened its own flight school at Luena, equipped with Cessna 172s.[5]

The crew of a Cuban-operated 23mm ZU-23-2 automatic gun. Like many Cuban anti-aircraft units deployed in Angola, this team consisted entirely of female operators. (Albert Grandolini Collection)

DAA Component

Atop of the flying branch operational since autumn 1975, the second element of the Angolan air force was meanwhile emerging in the form of ground-based air defences.[7] The background of this branch can be traced back to 1973 when the FAPLA Commander Eurico Manuel Correia Gonçalves underwent a course in anti-aircraft gunnery in North Korea, during which he was trained to use 14.5mm ZPU-1 heavy machine guns of Soviet origin. Once back in Angola, he trained a team of 12 militants, equipped with several 12.7mm DShK heavy machine guns. In June 1975, this team – meanwhile bolstered to 20 – was re-assigned to the cadre of the 9th Motorised Infantry Brigade (Brigada da Infantaria Motorizada, 9th BrIM), before 14 of its members were sent to Simferopol in the USSR for further training on 57mm S-60 towed automatic guns in September of the same year. Roughly around the same time, a single FAPLA officer was sent to Yugoslavia for a course on 20mm M55 anti-aircraft guns. Once everybody was back in Angola, late the same year, they established the Anti-Aircraft Company of the 9th BrIM. Reinforced by 30 further ranks trained in Guinea-Bissau – led by Agostinho José Neto 'Catete' – they installed all available M55s, ZPU-1s, ZPU-2s and ZPU-4s on Mercedes UNIMOG trucks, for improved mobility: together with the 9th BrIM, this unit subsequently took part in nearly all major ground warfare campaigns of late 1975 and early 1976. The officer trained in Yugoslavia was assigned to the Revolutionary Training Centre (Centro de Instrução Revolucionária, CIR) in Quiminha, and served as instructor for the Yugoslav-made anti-aircraft guns.[8]

It was around this cadre – once the operations against UNITA were concluded in mid-1976 – that the Anti-Aircraft Defence (Defesa Anti-Aviones, DAA) was established as a separate branch of the Angolan armed forces. Assigned to the command of 1st Lieutenant Paulo Sebastião 'Paulito', the DAA subsequently underwent rapid expansion. At first, it was reorganised into two sections: one for radar operations (Tropas Rádio Técnica), and one for operating anti-aircraft artillery and SAMs (Tropas de Artiharia Anti-Aérea e Foquetes), of which the latter was subdivided into four Anti-Aircraft Groups (Grupos de Artiharia Anti-Aerea, GAAA), each of which was equipped with a mix of truck-mounted 14.5mm ZPU-4 heavy machine guns and 23mm ZU-2 automatic anti-aircraft guns, and included a team equipped with Soviet-made 9K92M Strela-2M (ASCC/NATO-codename 'SA-7b Grail') man-portable air defence systems (MANPADs).[9]

FAPA/DAA

As of late 1976, only about 320 native Angolans served with the FAPA.[11] Nevertheless, more than 100 were already undergoing training abroad, and thousands were soon to follow. Encouraged, on 15 September the government in Luanda released a decree according to which the FAPA and the DAA were merged to become the FAPA/DAA and put under the overall command of Major Ciel da Conceição Cristóvão 'Gato'. Much more diligent than his predecessor, Gato quickly developed a plan to expand the air force and air defence force to a composition including:

- 2 fighter squadrons
- 1 transport squadron
- 1 reconnaissance and liaison squadron
- 1 SAM Brigade
- 2 radar battalions.[12]

In the fashion of prevalent overenthusiasm, the Ministry of Defence reacted on 12 October 1976, authorising Gato to establish the following units by 30 December 1976:

Table 5: DAA, Anti-Aircraft Units, 1977-1978[10]

GAAA	Operational Area	Equipment	Notes
1 GAAA	Luanda	ZU-23	18 guns organised into 3 batteries
2 GAAA	Luanda	M55	18 guns organised into 3 batteries
3 GAAA	Cabinda	ZU-23 & ZPU-4	4 pieces of each type, organised into 2 batteries
4 GAAA	Lobito	ZU-23 & ZPU-4	8 ZU-2 and 4 ZPU-4, organised into 3 batteries

- 1 squadron equipped with MiG-17s
- 1 squadron flying Mi-8 helicopters and An-26 transports
- 1 GAAA equipped with 20mm cannons
- 3 GAAAs operating a mix of ZU-23-2s and ZPU-4s by 30 December 1976.

Moreover, the same decree authorised Gato to establish five additional units by 30 December 1977, including:

- 1 light reconnaissance and liaison squadron
- 3 additional GAAAs equipped with ZU-23-2s and ZPU-4s
- 1 radar battalion

Finally, during the period between January 1979 and December 1980, the FAPA/DAA was to be further reinforced through the addition of the following units:

- 1 squadron equipped with MiG-17s
- 1 SAM-brigade (equipped with SA-3s)
- 2 GAAAs equipped with ZPU-4s and 37mm M1939/61-K automatic anti-aircraft guns
- 1 radar battalion

Based on this plan, hundreds of additional Angolan cadets were sent for training in the USSR, and a smaller number to Cuba, in 1976-1978.[13]

New Nests

Although Angola inherited a large network of airports and aerodromes from the Portuguese, the mass of these – especially facilities with military purposes as their primary and secondary task – were concentrated in northern and central Angola. On the contrary, like that of the entire FAPLA, the FAPA's threat assessments foremost concentrated on the south of the country. This in turn meant that the construction of numerous new – and dedicated – military air bases was necessary. The Ministry of Defence thus tasked the CO FAPA/DAA with finding suitable solutions. Following visits to Romania and Yugoslavia, Gato negotiated a contract with the Yugoslav company Planum Beograd for the construction of a large air base outside Lubango with two parallel runways and 28 blast pens, worth US$110 million. The resulting

Air Base No. 5 was not fully completed – only one runway was constructed to its full length, while the incomplete second served as a taxiway – on 3 August 1981, when the Cuban MiG-21 squadron moved in. Meanwhile, the Angolans had already contracted the Yugoslavs with the construction of the second – the Yuri Gagarin Air Base – outside Namibe.[14] Although a major runway there was constructed, for unknown reasons the rest of that project was never completed. Other airfields known to have been expanded through the late 1970s and early 1980s included Negage (which received 6 blast pens and an ammunition storage facility), Malanje (which received 10 blast pens), and Catumbela (which received 20 blast pens and underground depots for ammunition and fuel). Later on Cuban companies were contracted to expand and rebuild the airports of Huambo (which received 8 blast pens and underground storage facilities), and Luena, and to re-surface runways of Cuito Cuanavale, Matala, Menongue and several other airfields in order to make them better suitable for jet operations: older tarmac proved to be either 'aggressive' or of such bad quality, that jets like MiG-21s required the replacement of their tyres after every single sortie.[15]

What no expansion, construction or re-construction could solve was the fact that the majority of main air bases and airfields used by the DAA/FAR contingent in Angola, and the FAPA/DAA, were positioned high above sea level: for example, Xangongo at 1,250 metres (4,101ft), Menongue at 1,360m (4,462ft), and Lubango AB at no less than 1,760 metres (5,774ft). Indeed, even UNITA's main HQ in Jamba was at 1,460 metres (4,757ft) above sea level. Combined with high average ambient temperatures, operations from such airfields had detrimental effects upon performance of aircraft and helicopters: they decreased the maximum engine power on take-off while requiring higher speed of the take-off roll, and reduced the speed of climb. This in turn dictated all aircraft and helicopters to operate at reduced maximum take-off weights: i.e. they could carry less than if operated at lower altitudes above the sea.[16]

Radar Core

In February 1977, the FAPA/DAA received its first radars in the form of one P-15 Tropa (ASCC/NATO-codename 'Flat Face A') and one PRV-11 height-finder (ASCC/NATO-codename 'Side Net'). Later the same year, the unit operating these, the 1st Radar Company (officially established in January 1977)) was reinforced through the introduction to service of one P-37 Saturn (ASCC/NATO-

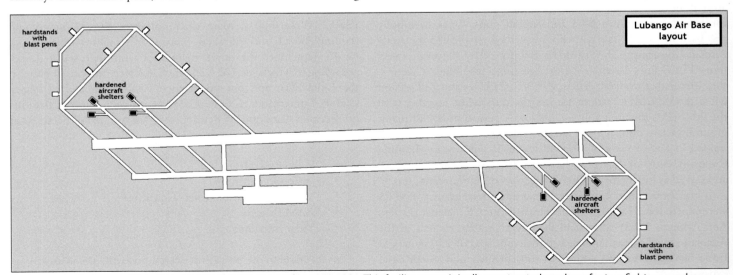

Basic layout of Lubango AB, constructed by Planum Beograd in 1979-1981. This facility was originally constructed as a base for two fighter squadrons, each of which received its complex of 10 hardstands protected by blast pens, and four hardened aircraft shelters to house jets standing quick reaction alert. By 1984, it was the home of two regiments with a total of six fighter squadrons. (Diagram by Tom Cooper)

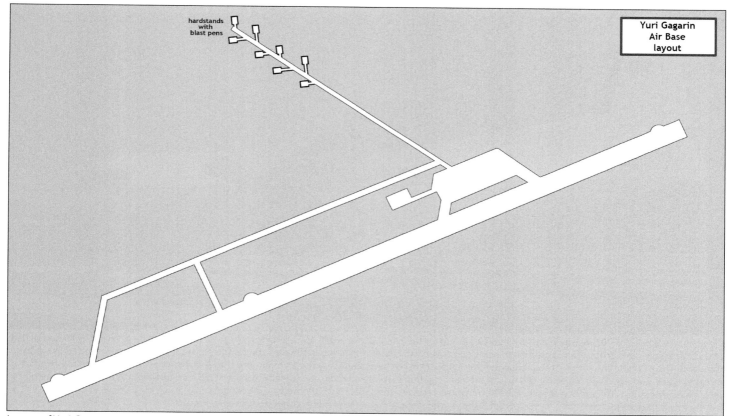

hardstands with blast pens

Yuri Gagarin Air Base layout

Layout of Yuri Gagarin AB constructed by the same Yugoslav company in the early 1980s. This facility was never completed and received only eight hardstands protected by blast pens, and two shelters for jets on alert duty. (Diagram by Tom Cooper)

Table 6: 1st Radar Battalion, FAPA/DAA, 1979[18]

Element	Operational Area	Equipment
1st Company	Mocamedes	PRV-11, P-12, P-15, P-37
2nd Company	Chibemba	PRV-11, P-12, P-15, P-37
3rd Company	Xamutete	P-12, P-15
4th Company	Menongue	PRV-11, P-12, P-15, P-37
5th Company	Lubango	PRV-11, P-12, P-15, P-37

codename 'Bar Lock') and one P-12 Yenisei (ASCC/NATO-codename 'Spoon Rest A') radar, the personnel for which were trained by members of the MMCA in Angola. The 2nd Radar Company was established at Lubango, in early 1978 and, upon return of additional specialists from training abroad in 1979 the 1st and 2nd Radar Companies were expanded into the 1st Radar Battalion: although this included 214 officers and other ranks that operated 16 radar systems organised and deployed as listed in Table 6, there were still not enough Angolan personnel available: until July 1979, at least two of the four companies of this battalion were staffed by the Cubans.[17]

Expanding Transport Capacity

The first group of Angolan pilots trained abroad returned to Luanda in mid-1978 – and was, once again, assigned to the Esquadron de Transportes. The same was true for most Angolan pilots who returned from training abroad in 1979: the first exception were seven pilots trained to fly An-2s and Yak-40s at the Aeroflot school in Kiev, who returned to Angola in December 1980. While all were initially assigned to the newly-established An-2 squadron, before long they were re-qualified to serve as instructor-pilots for Romanian-made IAR.823 basic trainers, and later also for Swiss-made Pilatus PC-7s (for details on both types, see below).[19]

The importance of the Esquadron de Transportes continued to grow over the following years as the worsening security situation in southern and central Angola left the FAPLA without the choice but to demand ever more support for garrisons isolated by UNITA's

A P-35 early warning radar and a PRV-11 height-finding radar, as seen in position outside Menongue airport. Taken from what appears to have been a trench nearby, this photograph is deceiving in so far as it does not show the elevated position of the two systems: both the P-35 and PRV-11 had to be emplaced atop at last an earthen mould to freely emit their electromagnetic energy, otherwise the ground reflection would oversaturate the radar. (Albert Grandolini Collection)

One of two Fokker F.27-200 maritime patrol aircraft acquired for the FAPA/DAA in 1978-1979. Due to its high acquisition cost – every F.27MPA was priced at US$25 million – this acquisition caused quite some controversy in Luanda, resulting in the decision for the second example to be outfitted as a pure transport. The example shown here thus remained the sole F.27MPA to be operated by the air force, and the FAPA/DAA never managed to fully exploit its capabilities. Equipped with an advanced instrumental navigation system and radar, it originally wore the civilian registration PH-FTU, before being re-serialled into R-301. The other example, used as transport, received the serial T-101. (Photo by Greg Meggs)

A rare photograph showing the other side of the same aircraft while airborne during pre-delivery testing. (Tom Cooper Collection)

operations. Moreover, because the FAPA/DAA was still lacking combat aircraft, it intensified the deployment of An-26s as bombers. Every example of this type was delivered together with four shackles for weapons of up to 500kg that could be installed on the lower central fuselage, and a glassed 'bulb' on the left side of the fuselage originally containing a visor used to 'aim' paradrops. Obviously, the latter also proved effective for aiming bombs. Contrary to Cuban-flown MiGs, the An-26 had the range to reach even Jamba, a village in the south-easternmost corner of Angola, which now crystallised as the new main base of UNITA. Jamba was subjected to regular air strikes, as recalled by one of the pilots involved:

Jamba was close to the border with Namibia, and thus we had to be cautious about South African interceptors. Therefore, whenever flying for Jamba, we launched from Menongue, crossed over southwest Zambia, and then attacked from the east – which was an unexpected direction of approach. Up to three MiG-17Fs would escort us on the way in and on return, as their range allowed.[20]

With some five or six An-26s almost constantly busy flying air strikes, the Esquadron de Transportes had to be reinforced by additional aircraft. Therefore, in 1978-1979 it received all the Alouette helicopters originally operated by the Cubans, and then two Lockheed L-100-30 Hercules transports and the first of two Fokker F.27 maritime patrol aircraft.[21]

Excessive Attrition

As the operations of transport aircraft intensified, attrition became high – both to accidents and in combat. Indeed, it seems that virtually all of the first batch of 11 An-26s were written off within less than six years. For example, an An-26 was hit by an RPG-7 while taking off from Cuangar on 12 June 1977. The crew – including pilot Fernando José Pereira Jardim Ferreira, and co-pilot Euclides Rosario Oliveira – managed an emergency landing in open savannah outside the airfield, but the aircraft had to be abandoned there. How dangerous strike sorties against UNITA's bases in the south-eastern corner of Angola could get became obvious on 7 November 1980,

One of two Lockheed L-100-30 Hercules acquired by Angola in 1978: although both wore civilian livery and markings, they were almost exclusively deployed for the support of the FAPLA. (Albert Grandolini Collection)

Another acquisition for the FAPA/DAA was this Tupolev Tu-134 airliner, equipped as a VIP transport and used for carrying top officials around the country and on visits abroad. (Tom Cooper Collection)

when an An-26 piloted by Francisco Tavares de Almeida, with Arnaldo da Fonseca Diupré, was shot down by a SAAF Impala while underway from Mucusse to Cuando-Cubango loaded with FAB-500 bombs. Another transport of the same type – a TAAG-operated aircraft wearing civilian registration D2-EPQ – was shot down by a SA-7 south of Vila Nova de Armada on 15 or 22 November 1980 (sources differ), killing the crew consisting of the pilot Mário Gonçalves Coelho and co-pilot Flávio Alves Cardoso. Only a week later, a third An-26 was shot down by UNITA's MANPADs, and two of its Soviet crew – including pilot Kamilo Abdurahmanovic Molayev and loadmaster Ivan Chernietsky – were captured.[22]

A fifth An-26 went missing in the Licua area in 1981, the sixth disappeared on a flight from Luena to Luanda, in the same year, and the sole Angolan Lockheed L-100-20 Hercules (registered as D2-EAS) was shot down only six kilometres outside Menongue on 16 May 1981, killing the crew of four.[23] Further An-26 losses are known to have occurred on 7 June 1982 in the Lubango area (where the aircraft piloted by Cuban Captain Osvaldo Lopes Torrero was shot down), on 29 November 1982 (see below for details), on 24 December 1982 (when UNITA shot down an aircraft that was about to land in Lupire), and two in 1983, when the An-26 piloted by Sául Pereira e Francisco Chagas was shot down over Jamba, while another aircraft was written off in Cangamba (see below for further details).[24] Meanwhile, the remaining Noratlases were worn out to a degree where they had to be withdrawn from service in 1982. The

type was replaced by additional An-26s (a total of 22 of which were acquired by 1987), which prompted the FAPA/DAA to split the Esquadron de Transportes into three units:

- 1 Esquadron 'Quissonde'
- 2 Esquadron
- 3 Esquadron 'VIP'[25]

Cooperation with Airlines

Heavy tasking of the sole transport wing of the FAPA/DAA, and continuous attrition eventually resulted in the FAPLA requesting support from the national airliner TAAG. The original five Boeing 737-200s of this company – delivered to Angola once Washington had issued special permission, starting with 3 March 1976 – began carrying troops and supplies around the country in 1980. Meanwhile, another Angolan airline became involving in supporting the FAPLA: this was the Consortio Technico de Aeronautica (CTA), established in 1978. Its Boeing 707s and the sole Lockheed L-100-20 Hercules, were primarily used to haul jet fuel to various airports and air bases around the country. While CTA ceased operating in 1979, TAAG subsequently found itself on the receiving end of several insurgent attacks. On 8 November 1983, its Boeing 737-200 registered as D2-TBN was hit by an SA-7 MANPAD of the FALA, shortly after taking-off from Lubango airport: the aircraft was only 60 metres (200ft) above the ground when it received a hit, which caused it to veer to the left and hit the ground, only 800 metres past the runway. All four crewmembers and 126 passengers were killed. Concerned about negative publicity, Luanda subsequently declared a 'technical failure' as the cause of the crash. Nothing of that kind could have been done on 9 February 1984, when a bomb placed by UNITA operatives destroyed the hydraulic lines of the Boeing 737-200 registered as D2-TBV, minutes after a take-off from Huambo airport. The crew managed to return for an emergency landing but overran the runway by 80 metres and the aircraft was subsequently written off. Fortunately, thanks to a swift evacuation, none of the 6 crewmembers and 136 passengers was injured.[26]

The Workhorse

In 1978, the FAPA/DAA was supposed to have its first Mi-8T unit established: this plan was not realised although the second batch of 12 such helicopters (28 of which were eventually acquired) was in the country by that time – in addition to the four Mi-8Ts brought to Angola by the Cubans in 1975 (H-01, H-02, H-03, and H-04). The reason was that the first group of 15 cadets trained on the type returned from training in the USSR only in May 1979.[27]

Members off the MMCA in front of the Mi-8T H-02 – one of the first four helicopters of this type, brought to Angola by the Cubans. (via Albert Grandolini)

Cuban commandos disembarking from Mi-8T H-03, probably the only helicopter of this type in Angola to receive a camouflage pattern. (via Albert Grandolini)

Therefore, additional helicopters were initially only operated by Cubans and Soviets. One of them – serial H-06 – was shot down by the FNLA, on 17 May 1978: although the crew landed safely, all three were summarily executed by the insurgents. One of the 12 Mi-8s delivered in 1976 – serial number H-14 – was equipped as a VIP-transport. Recognisable by its square windows, it was initially flown by Soviet crews only and frequently carried President dos Santos. Two other Mi-8Ts (including one example that was painted in orange overall and registered as CCCP-22581l), were always operated by the Soviets.[28]

While then working up the resulting unit – the Luanda IAP-based Esquadra de Helicópteros Mi-8 – in 1979, the Angolans were quick to find out that it was severely underpowered. Especially during operations from airfields positioned relatively high above sea level in central Angola, like those in Huambo, Bié, Luena or Menongue, crews of the FAPA/DAA were forced to the conclusion that only rolling take-offs were possible, especially when the helicopter was fully loaded (its maximum capacity was 20-25 fully equipped soldiers, for example). Nevertheless, the type was enthusiastically accepted by its crews. When the unit, initially commanded by

Captain Domingos Adriano da Silva Neto 'Simy', experienced its first accident – in the Vila Nova de Armada (Cuando-Cubango province) in 1979 – it was because one of three Mi-8Ts underway by night crashed on landing as its pilot became disoriented.[29]

Subsequently, Mi-8s became the work-horses of the FAPA/DAA: they were deployed in support of virtually every operation of the FAPLA and the MMCA/FAR in Angola, and in a host of operations run by the air force only. Partially because of training systems run by Soviet instructors and criticised by the Angolans as 'irresponsible', the fleet suffered horrendous losses: well over 100 accidents and incidents involving Mi-8Ts are known to have taken place by 1987, and it is certain that every single helicopter of this type operated by Angolan and Cuban crews received a degree of combat damage on one or another occasion: several helicopters repeatedly. Eight losses occurred during the early 1980s: on 3 November 1981, the Mi-8T serial number H-45 – relatively fresh from repairs after combat damage it had received about a year before – was underway on a liaison mission from Huambo to Menongue, piloted by Captain Lourenço Kitumba Júnior. While crossing over the Bié area, the helicopter was shot down by small-arms fire and crashed, killing the entire crew. The FAPA/DAA deployed another Mi-8T – H-07, piloted by Domingos Teófilo da Costa Gika – two Alouette IIIs and at least one MiG-17F to search for possible survivors. Shortly after finding the wreckage of the downed H-45, H-07 received small-arms hits into both engines. In panic, its pilot jumped overboard, thus *de-facto* committing a suicide. However, the co-pilot retained his nerves and made an emergency landing: he and the other two crewmembers were then recovered by one of the Alouette IIIs, all uninjured.[30]

One of the Romanian-manufactured IAR.316B Alouettes of the FAPA/DAA (serial number H-227), in flight during the late 1980s. (via Albert Grandolini)

Another Mi-8T was lost while piloted by the Cuban Raúl Vigo, on 23 August 1982: it was shot down – probably by an SA-7 – with the loss of everybody on board. On 6 November 1982, the Cuban-operated H-09 was shot down near Baixo Longa in Cuando-Cubango province, with the loss of three crew and 12 passengers. Only the co-pilot was recovered alive. On 8 August 1983, and as described in *Volume 2*, another Cuban-operated Mi-8T was hit by ground fire during the Battle of Cangamba: although its pilot, Major Policarpo Alvarez Pileta was killed, the co-pilot managed to fly it safely back to base. On 29 December 1983, another Cuban-operated Mi-8T – piloted by Lieutenant Armando Jesus Galindo Bacallo – was shot down in the Luau area, with the loss of everybody on board. Finally, on 12 January 1984, a Mi-8T piloted by Lieutenant-Colonel Albizu exploded in flight while loaded with 'do-it-yourself' napalm bombs and underway to attack an insurgent position, killing all five on board.[31]

Western Aircraft

The other FAPA/DAA helicopter asset underwent an entirely different experience. In 1976, the first Angolan crew for Alouette III helicopters, led by former MPLA guerrillero João Gonçalves Fortunato, was qualified to operate the type. Although an SE.316B was then lost in an accident – grievously injuring the co-pilot, Joaquim Jacinto Quental – the Angolans were highly satisfied, and thus a group of cadets was sent to Portugal for training on Alouettes in the same year. On their return and using the two Alouette II Lamas and five Alouette IIIs originally operated by the Cubans, they established the Esquadra de Alouette, commanded by Gonçalves Fortunato, as a sub-unit of the Esquadron de Transportes. While Gonçalves Fortunato was advanced in rank and replaced by Major José Ramalho Gomes in 1977, the Angolans remained pleased with the type and a year later sent another group of pilots for training in Portugal, while acquiring additional Alouettes via the national oil company, Sonangol.[32]

The popularity of the Alouette reached such proportions that the Angolans became keen to repeat the Rhodesian and South African practices of deploying these as gunships. Therefore, they attempted to acquire German-made 20mm MG.151 automatic cannons: this effort proved largely fruitless. Eventually, only three MG.151s were purchased from Portuguese stocks. Even then, these were promptly installed into the rear cabins of three Alouettes, converting them into gunships capable of providing fire-support. The Angolans then flight-tested an alternative in the form of the Soviet-made AGS-17

Soviet advisors inspecting the installation of a MG.151 gun on one of FAPA/DAA's Alouette IIIs. (via Albert Grandolini)

grenade-launcher: however, due to strong vibrations, this weapon proved impossible to aim precisely, and this effort was abandoned.[33]

Nevertheless, the Alouette remained highly popular and thus in 1980 Angola placed an order for 21 IAR.316Bs (in Project Misunea Secreta Sirius) – a version manufactured in Romania under licence. After an additional group of Angolan pilots underwent a conversion course in that country, the first of these reached Luanda in July 1981, and were pressed into service with the ENAM (see below for details), to be used for training of further pilots and ground crews. The Romanian-manufactured examples arrived equipped to carry up to four Soviet-designed UB-16-57 pods for 57mm S-5 rockets, but these proved inadequate for Angolan requirements, and were never used in combat. Instead, later on crews of what had meanwhile expanded into the Escuadrillha Alouette began installing Soviet-made B-8M pods for 80mm S-8 unguided rockets on their machines.[34]

Angolan PC-7 pilots with one of their Soviet instructors in 1984-1985. Notable is that while the aircraft in the foreground of this photograph wore camouflage colours, the one to the rear was left in civilian livery and wore a civilian registration – although obviously armed with the same 90mm rocket pods serving with the FAPA/DAA. (via Albert Grandolini)

A pair of Soviet advisors in front of a BN-2 operated by the FAPA/DAA in the late 1970s. (via Albert Grandolini)

two other BN-2s were written off at unknown dates in 1983 and 1984, and both of their pilots killed.[36]

Islanders continued serving as light transports and for reconnaissance purposes until 1984, when they were replaced by 12 Pilatus PC-7s, ordered in 1981 – and then against Cuban advice (MMCA and DAA/FAR officers would have preferred the Czechoslovak-made Aero L-39ZA Albatross, an armed variant of the well-known jet trainer). In November of the same year, 2nd Lieutenants Júlio Leitão and Hélder da Silva Ramos (both of whom had served with TAAG until that time) travelled to Switzerland for a 45-day-long conversion course, together with Captain Adriano António Neto de Carvalho, a technician. Back in Angola, they ran a conversion course for a group of about a dozen additional pilots and a similar number of technicians that, once the first PC-7s reached Angola, in 1982, established the Esquadron de Reconhecimento e Assalto, the first commander of which was 2nd Lieutenant Manuel Aguiar de Matos. By this time, four additional pilots are known to have been undergoing conversion training in Switzerland. While home-based at Luanda IAP, the unit usually operated multiple small detachments at airfields closer to the combat zone, and its aircraft were deployed not only for reconnaissance and attack, but also as flying command posts and radio-relays. Angolan PC-7s were usually armed with pods for 90mm unguided rockets made by FN of Belgium, and deployed – often in association with Alouette helicopters – to search for and attack insurgent camps.[37]

Strategic Disagreement

As can be seen from the descriptions above, by 1979-1980, the FAPA/DAA was busy expanding its transport capabilities and its ground-based air defences. On the contrary, the plan for the establishment of just one MiG-17-squdaron was lagging well behind the schedule. Certainly enough, the first group of pilots qualified to fly MiG-17Fs returned from training in the USSR in the summer of 1979: however, nothing is known to have happened for the next few months. While Angolan sources are silent about the reason, Trujillo Hernández left no doubts: 'They came back from training in the Soviet Union…. begun to create combat units, but were in a very difficult position, and suffered human and equipment losses. The Angolan personnel were not ready, technically and sociologically.'[38]

Meanwhile, in 1978 Angola acquired four British-made Britten-Norman BN-2A-21 Islanders for the civilian authorities. In 1980, these were reinforced by four and then eight additional examples manufactured under licence in Romania, and then transferred to the newly established Esquadra de Reconhecimento, and operated by its sub-unit, the Esqudrillha de Islander. This unit became the only asset of the FAPA/DAA to ever deploy chemical weapons at war: in 1983, it was used to deploy defoliants against farms in UNITA-controlled areas where food for the insurgency was produced.[35]

Initially commanded by Lieutenant Kanga José, the Esquadra de Reconhecimento experienced several losses during the first few years of its operations. On 9 June 1981, one of ENAM's BN-2s – serial I-302 – disappeared over the Nova Caipemba area, in the Uige province, while searching for a Soviet-owned and flown Mi-8T painted orange overall but wearing the Aeroflot markings and the Soviet registration CCCP-22581. No trace of either aircraft was found ever again, despite intensive search and rescue operations including an Angolan Lama and several other aircraft. Another BN-2 – though this time crewed by the Romanians – lost its way during a flight from Negage and made an emergency landing inside Zaire in 1982: its crew was returned only months later. Finally,

Moreover, according to official Cuban sources, there was a major disagreement over the strategy between Havana and Luanda. The Cubans envisaged the deployment of the MMCA as a deterrent and defence against a possible invasion from abroad, and in an advisory role. Correspondingly, in the course of a series of offensives run in 1978-1979, the MMCA managed to not only work up a number of FAPLA's COIN units to a reasonable level of efficiency but to demolish UNITA once again. However, stubbornly following Soviet advice, the MPLA continued insisting on the build-up of its conventional forces, and on keeping its best units away from COIN operations. Moreover, the senior leadership in Luanda began developing resentments not only vis-à-vis the influence of the Cuban military but also of civilian advisors and began acting without even informing them. In 1977 and 1978, it permitted two major attacks by Katangan insurgents into Zaire (affairs known as Shaba I and Shaba II), creating tensions with their northern neighbour, and in 1978 run an anti-UNITA offensive without consulting the MMCA. Already considering the MPLA's conduct of the war at the strategic level to be a massive mistake, the Cubans were incensed to a degree where they completely stopped their COIN effort: they withdrew their entire specialised COIN-asset, the Regiment for Combat against Mercenary Bands (Regimento de Lucha Contra Bandas Mercenarias) and all COIN-advisors from FAPLA units, and, in March 1979, all the MMCA units deployed in southern Angola were withdrawn back to the Fidel Castro Line.

By the time it was handed over to the FAPA/DAA, the sole MiG-15UTI ever delivered to Angola had received a similar camouflage pattern to the MiG-17Fs and was assigned the serial C01. It is seen here rolling down the tarmac at Lubango AB, prior to the next training sortie, in 1979 or 1980. (via Luis Dominguez)

A group of Cuban instructors waiting for their Angolan students prior to the next training flight on MiG-17F serial number C24 in 1980-1981. (Albert Grandolini Collection)

One of 12 IAR.823s Angola acquired from Romania in 1980-1981. They served as basic trainers at the ENAM and were used to train hundreds of future pilots and ground personnel of the FAPA/DAA. (via Albert Grandolini)

Working-up of the Angolan MiG-17 unit thus advanced very slowly. The original Cuban unit – commanded by Major José Montes – did hand over all of the nine surviving MiG-17Fs and one MiG-15UTI, and then helped complete the training of Angolan pilots and ground personnel, but it was only in early 1980 that the unit commanded by Captain Francisco Lopes Gonçalves Afonso 'Hanga' was declared operational. Almost immediately, Hanga received the order to re-deploy his squadron from Luanda IAP to the newly constructed Yuri Gagarin AB, and provide support for the Operation code-named Red May. However, Hanga's pilots were not the experienced Cubans, and at the time the FAPA/DAA still had no operational radar network covering all of Angolan air space. Thus, the limitations of MiG-17Fs and their inexperienced pilots

A fully bombed-up Mirage F.1AZ seen prior to its next mission, on the tarmac of Ondangva AB. With the Angolan SAM-threat still being low, and distances to the target zone within easy reach at this time in the war, South African Mirages still frequently flew carrying up to eight Mk.82s. This practice had to be discontinued later during the war. (SAAF)

A pair of trucks carrying V-601 missiles of the S-125/SA-3 system, in a parade in Luanda in the early 1980s. (Albert Grandolini Collection)

saw its first action in 1979, when one of its units claimed a 'Mirage' (probably a Mirage IIIRZ or IIIR2Z underway on a reconnaissance mission) as shot down in the area south-east of Lubango. However, the SAAF is not known to have suffered any such loss: indeed, available South African sources do not even indicate knowledge about the presence of any SA-3s near the areas where the SAAF operated for almost a year longer.[3]

In 1980, the FAPA/DAA re-deployed one of the combat groups of the 40th BDAA for protection of the construction site of the Yuri Gagarin AB, and the 5th Company of the 1st Radar Battalion to Lubango, where this served to form the core of the future 2nd Radar Battalion. A delivery of four additional SA-3 systems (together with another 144 V-601 operational missiles and a total of 37 training rounds) enabled the creation of the 14th Combat Group of the 40th BDAA, and establishment of the 50th BDAA with three combat groups. However, according to Cuban sources, the Angolans were so critically short of personnel for all of this equipment, that even as of 1981-1983 only two of the 40th and 50th's combat groups were operated by FAPA/DAA personnel, supervised by the Soviets: the other four (including two protecting Lubango and two in Matala) were all staffed by the Cubans.[4]

Pechora units in Angola were to see their first action before long – and then because the South Africans were also undergoing their own learning process. In reaction to a series of SWAPO attacks, on 7 June 1980 the SADF launched the Operations Smokeshell and Sceptic: one element of these was a massive air strike on SWAPO's Tobias Haneko training camp, situated in the outskirts of Lubango. This undertaking was proceeded by a reconnaissance sortie flown by a single Mirage IIIR2Z, escorted by a pair of Mirage F.1CZs. Rather unsurprisingly, the French-made BF1 radar-warning receivers of all three jets warned their pilots about emissions by SA-

Correspondingly, all the available GAAAs were re-deployed to positions in Benguela, Namibe, Xangongo, and Ongiva. Moreover, two reinforced GAAAs (both equipped with Czechoslovak-made 30mm M53/59 anti-aircraft guns) were established for the defence of Lubango and Cahama, and another two (both equipped with Yugoslav-made M55s) in Xangongo and Ongiva. Finally, to replace units sent south, a battery equipped with Soviet-made 37mm M1939s was established in Chibemba, and another GAAA equipped with 30mm M53/59s at Luanda IAP.[2]

Furthermore, Luanda secured a major reinforcement for the FAPA/DAA in the form of its first heavy SAM-systems. After a suitably sized group of cadets underwent training in the USSR, and once the 1st Radar Battalion was in operational condition, in April 1979 the Soviets delivered of the first three S-125 Pechora heavy SAM systems. These arrived accompanied by 108 V-601 missiles and one Akkord 75A/125A symulation system (used for training crews). The personnel and equipment in question were organised into the 40th Anti-Aircraft Missile Brigade (Brigada de Defesa Anti-Aérea, BDAA), which consisted of three (later four) battalions or SAM sites: designated 'combat groups', they were numbered from 11 to 13. According to Angolan sources, the 40th BDAA

3s as they flashed low above the Lubango area around 13.00hrs, taking photographs of the training camp and the nearby air base.[5] However, the low-altitude of their appearance took the Cubans by surprise, and nobody fired back. The latter fact prompted the SAAF planners to draw a wrong conclusion: supposedly, the Angolans had not yet loaded any missiles on their launchers, or otherwise they would open fire. Correspondingly, 16 Mirage F.1AZs and F.1CZs were launched from Ondangwa AB in northern South West Africa into an attack even before the photographs taken by the Mirage IIIR2Z could be developed. The four flights of four jets each flew well to

Cuban and Angolan operators of an SA-3 site. Visible in the foreground are a pair of V.601 missiles (both already well-weathered after being exposed to the local elements for some time). Visible in the right background is the antenna of the SRN-125 'Low Blow' fire-control radar: one of two centrepieces of every SA-3 SAM site. (Albert Grandolini Collection)

the west of Lubango, before turning around to attack from the north towards the south: in this fashion, they took the SA-3 crews by surprise once again, and no missiles were fired at them during their low-altitude approach, or as the first two flights delivered their attack. However, one Mirage from the third flight was narrowly missed by at least one V-601, and two jets from the fourth flight were damaged by several others. By the time the SAAF formation withdrew towards the south, two MiG-21MFs had been scrambled from Cubango: however, these proved unable to catch the low-flying Mirages. This first South African experience with SA-3s

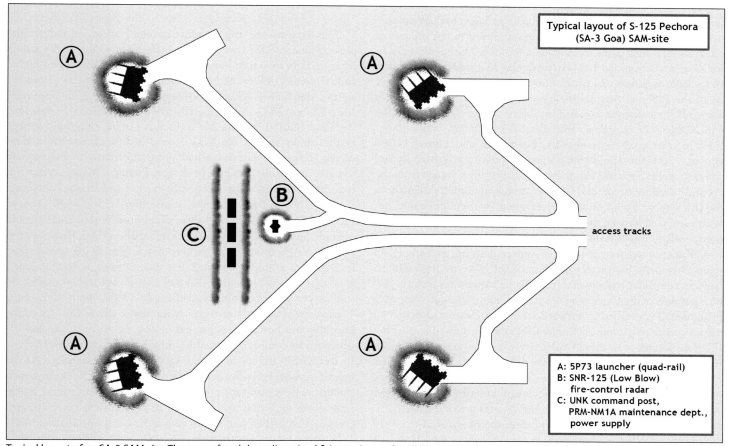

Typical layout of an SA-3 SAM site. The core of each battalion-sized firing unit was the UNK command post and the SNR-125/Low Blow fire-control radar. Supported by power supply and maintenance departments, the UNK command post exercised control over the Low Blow and four 5P73 quadruple launchers for V-601 missiles. Usually, all the elements were surrounded by earthen berms for protection against air and artillery attacks. Notably, it is possible that the Angolans applied the same approach to their acquisition of SA-3s as, for example, Algeria and Iraq, which equipped each of their SAM sites of this type with just three 5P73 quadruple launchers. (Diagram by Tom Cooper)

thus ended in a shock, and two Mirage F.1AZs (234 and 237) made emergency landings back in SWA.[6]

IFF Problems

Unknown to the South Africans was the fact that the Pechora crews at Lubango remained on alert for days longer: the tension reached such a proportion that on 8 June 1980 one of the Cuban crews of the 40th BDAA misidentified a Yak-40 of the TAAG underway from Huambo to Lubango, and shot it down with a V-601 over Matala, killing all 32 on board, including the Soviet crew of the jet: pilot Valery Angurov, co-pilot Vyacheslav Krylov, and navigator Vasily Golubev.[7] The Cuban SA-3 crews made three further mistakes of a similar kind: in addition to one in 1981 (see below for details), they shot down the sole An-26 operated by the DAA/FAR contingent near Lubango, and on 29 November 1982 their SA-3s shot down the sole An-26 operated by the TAAG at the time. Registered as D2-TAB, the latter aircraft was underway from Lubango to Namibe and was shot down over Monte Bibala. That accident resulted in the death of a Soviet crew – including pilot Nikolai Fyodorovich Kusch, co-pilot Eugeniy Krasavin, navigator Anush Kakoyan, and radio-operator Anatoliy Alekseev – and 11 passengers.[8]

These four incidents exposed another major issue relating to the operation of radar-guided SAMs and an integrated air defence network (IADS) of the kind the Angolans were in the process of establishing at least to protect the Lubango area. The operation of an IADS, and radar-guided SAMs in particular, required the installation and proper function of identification friend or foe (IFF) systems. As of the 1980s in Angola, IFF-systems consisted of two primary elements: a transceiver installed into radars – like the P-19 Danube (ASCC/NATO-codename 'Flat Face B') – which could either listen to or trigger a response from; and a transponder installed into aircraft. The latter would emit a signal identifying it as friendly and showing its bearing, and also helped to determine its range from the ground-based interrogator. However, and despite their designation, the IFF systems could only positively identify friendly targets, not hostile ones. Moreover, they could not positively identify aircraft the transponders of which did not reply (because they were turned off or malfunctioning, for example), or were responding with an invalid reply. Obviously, the proper function of IFF systems depended on flawless coordination between multiple headquarters: because IFF transponders of the time could be set only before take-off, if the HQ of the IADS had failed to forward valid identification codes to all parties concerned, if one of these failed to receive it on time, or if the IFF transponder of an aircraft failed to reply in the expected fashion, it could happen all too easily that a friendly aircraft was misidentified as a foe, and it would be fired upon. This was even more important considering that the SRN-125 fire control radar of the SA-3 SAM systems in Angola during the 1980s had no means to interrogate IFF of any kind of aircraft: they depended on the operator of the P-19 early warning radars informing them correctly about the identity of the targets they were tracking.[9]

The position of the Cuban-manned Radio-Technical unit in Huambo in the early 1980s. Barely visible is the PRV-11 hight-finding radar on the left, and a P-19 radar in the centre. (via Luis Dominguez)

People's Supersonic Jets

In Angola of 1981 – a country that six years earlier was released into independence while having only about 50 qualified medical doctors – there was only a very rudimentary radar network to support SAM operators, and to guide pilots and help them navigate, and very few radio beacons. Alex Diaz, a former ground controller of the DAA/FAR, recalled:

In Angola, we had only primary radars to control the airspace and help our pilots navigate. Such as P-19, P-37, PRV-13 (height-finder) and two RSP-10s used for approach and landing. Our pilots sometimes used commercial radio beacons, however, they mostly required support from ground control. Indeed, the ground control was most important: pilots had to follow my commands all the time.[10]

The reasons for this modus operandi were related to the previously mentioned way the GenStab expected the Soviet armed forces to fight their next war, and thus the way the GenStab equipped and trained its officers and other ranks. The main types of combat aircraft the USSR delivered to Angola between 1975-1984 were MiG-17s and MiG-21s. Originally based on the MiG-15 of Korean War fame (1950-1953), the MiG-17F was a significant improvement of the earlier model: the MiG-15 was a difficult aircraft at high speeds and was an equally difficult gun platform due to its tendency to snake and pitch. Having a re-designed wing of bigger surface but reduced thickness, and a new tailfin on a longer fuselage containing the Klimov VK-1 engine with an afterburner, MiG-17F showed much better behaviour in all these disciplines, and became capable of safely breaking the sound barrier in a shallow dive. However, the jet was designed with interception of bombers flying straight and level at high altitudes in mind. For this purpose, it was equipped with two 23mm Nudelman-Rikhter NR-23 autocannons with 80 rounds per gun, and one Nudelman N-37 gun with 40 rounds. These were relatively heavy guns with a slow rate of fire – good for knocking out bombers, as proven during the Korean War, but ill-suited for air combat against small, nimble and manoeuvring targets. In the USSR and allied countries, the type was relegated to the fighter-bomber role after becoming obsolete in the 1960s: however, even if its three cannons proved highly effective in ground attack, now it was suffering from the lack of capability to carry a useful combination of fuel and underwing armament. Specifically, MiG-17Fs delivered to Angola were equipped with add-on underwing hardpoints enabling them to carry UB-16-57 pods for 57mm S-5K unguided rockets *in addition* to two 400-lite underwing drop tanks: if any rocket pods or bombs were installed, then these were *in place* of the drop tanks. In such configuration, their range was limited to about 150 kilometres (93 miles).

While its designation and purpose might stipulate something else, the MiG-21 was an entirely different type of aircraft. Like the MiG-17, it was a high-altitude interceptor, however, it was also capable of reaching Mach 2 and climbing higher and faster than its predecessor. Moreover, while striving to pack so much performance into a simple and lightweight airframe that could also be operated under austere conditions, in the case of the MiG-21 the designers sacrificed almost everything – especially firepower and endurance. No matter how much it was intended to correct the numerous deficiencies in regards of range and weaponry of the earlier variants, the MiG-21MFs delivered to Angola in early 1976 offered only a slight improvement. The Tumansky R-13 engine was more powerful; internal fuel capacity was slightly improved; there was an internally installed 23mm twin-barrel GSh-23 cannon with 250 rounds, and there were blown flaps for improved low-speed manoeuvrability. The principal actual improvement was the availability of four (instead of the original two) underwing hardpoints: as well as carrying R-3S (ASCC/NATO-codename 'AA-2 Atoll') infra-red homing air-to-air missiles, these could also carry bombs up to 500kg, or rocket pods like the UB-16-57 and UB-32-57 for 57mm S-5K unguided rockets. Moreover, the outer pair of underwing hardpoints was plumbed for carriage of 400-litre drop tanks instead of bombs, missiles or rockets, and another drop tank of the same capacity could be installed under the centreline hardpoint. However, navigational aids of the MiG-21MF were as austere as those of the MiG-17F, while the view outside the cockpit was much worse, and the Tumansky R-13 engine was thirsty during operations at low altitude, limiting the effective range under operational war-loads to slightly over 200 kilometres (124 miles). Except for the most experienced pilots, anybody flying it was even more dependant upon good ground control for flying effective combat operations.

Overall, both types – MiG-17F and MiG-21MF – lacked the endurance, the payload-range combination, and manoeuvrability necessary to fight a COIN war. As the wars in the Middle East of the 1967-1973 period showed, they were underdogs in comparison to older French-made jets like the Dassault Mirage IIICZ/EZ operated by the SAAF: the air battles of 1981 and 1982 showed that MiG-21MFs were no match for more advanced Mirage F.1s either. Both of the Soviet-built aircraft lacked sophisticated sensors and navigation equipment and their pilots depended on precise guidance from the ground for effective operations.

Peculiarities of the Soviet and Cuban Training System

The Soviet pilot and SAM operator training syllabuses were based on the assumption that the cadet had no understanding of combat aircraft and their armament at all, and on the assumption that there was no other way for cadets to learn than through repetitive instruction. This instruction took time resulting in a training system in which the pilot progressed at a slow pace. On average, Angolan cadets would spend three years in the USSR: the first year was spent learning the Russian language and undergoing theoretical courses, and it was only towards its end that they would receive pre-flight instruction. Flying commenced at the start of the second year: it included about 60 hours of elementary flight training, followed by a 90 hour jet flight training course, most of which consisted of rather short flights in Czechoslovak-made Aero L-29 Delfins and L-39 Albatrosses. Finally, a future fighter pilot would receive about 100 hours on the MiG-15UTI two-seat conversion trainer and MiG-17 single-seater. It was only at this point in time that Angolan cadets

would start a direct conversion to MiG-21s. During that course, they received lots of theoretical training, but were taught to fly only take-offs and landings, very basic ground attacks, and next to no air combat manoeuvring – all of this only in clear weather and always within the sight of the home base. As for all Soviet cadets, their upgrade to mission-ready status would then take an additional three years and 350-400 hours of flight training – just to be cleared for day-only combat operations – and another year or two and 450-500 hours to be cleared for night alert duties and supervised ground attack or air combat operations. Overall, the Soviet training system took seven to eight years to produce a fully qualified combat pilot. Even then, to save cost and minimize risks, this training system was strictly limited by exaggerated safety measures and severe penalties for any departure from the predetermined procedure. As a result, even fully qualified pilots never learned how to operate their aircraft to their limits.[11]

At least in theory, building-up an integrated air defence system (IADS) might appear to have been a much quicker process. For example, in Syria in 1973, about 3,000 Soviet advisors took only six months to literally jump-start an air defence force operating more than 100 radar stations and SAM sites, networked into an IADS.[12] However, contrary to Angola, Syria had enough experienced personnel with the necessary qualifications: the Angolans first had to provide elementary education to their future pilots, technicians, electricians, and radar and SAM operators, before sending them for military education abroad. Moreover, and as the Angolans were to learn over time, even if the Soviet weapon systems were cheap to acquire and relatively simple to operate, and the Soviets were usually much quicker in delivering than any Western competition could, and although the Soviets were ready to provide training services to their foreign customers at attractive terms, the overall combat value of the equipment and training they were providing did not match that of their Western competition. Overall, Soviet weapons systems – and their operators – functioned well only after a lengthy process of working up, and then if operated as a part of a well-developed IADS, commanded by a versed commander. The system worked either poorly, or not at all if these conditions were not present and there was relatively little even a versed pilot or SAM operator could change about this. Regardless of how optimistic they were at the start of building-up their air force, the Angolans had to learn numerous bitter lessons first. All of these issues – Soviet and Cuban training methods, limitations of the Soviet-made equipment including both aircraft and air-defence systems – were to play their role in the next series of crucial experiences of the Cuban and Angolan air power during the War of Intervention.

Bitter Complaints

Considering all described above, it is unsurprising that the Angolans were quick to grow disappointed with the armament and services provided by the USSR. Indeed, they were not the only ones to complain about the Soviet training methods. Lieutenant-Colonel Manuel Rojas Garcia – a DAA/FAR MiG-21 pilot shot down and captured by UNITA in 1988 – observed:

In the USSR, Soviet instructors were strictly following their planning, and all were absolutely determined to fulfil their norms. A failure to do so would have been understood as their failure. Thus, they frequently graduated young people who lacked skills and capabilities necessary to fly fighter jets….to avoid catastrophic accidents, they taught cadets only the most basic things, and avoided any kind of complex exercises. The result was that cadets that came back to Angola knew only how to take-off and land: they lacked even the knowledge necessary for us to then take over and further improve their skills. However, we had no time: we had to work them up and send them into combat operations against the guerrillas – under challenging geographic and climatic conditions, and in aircraft not designed for COIN warfare. Unsurprisingly, losses in pilots, aircraft and helicopters – most caused by pilot-errors, loss of orientation, and similar – were much too frequent.'[13]

The first Angolan fighter-jet unit, a squadron of the 26th RACB that used to operate MiG-17Fs (all of which were still the same jets delivered in late 1975 and then operated by the Cubans), was effectively disbanded in 1983 following a series of fatal incidents. Most of its mounts were abandoned where they had been parked for the last time: this was C24, as left at the airport of Cuito Cuanavale. (Albert Grandolini Collection)

If the quality of training of FAPA/DAA cadets in the USSR was disappointing for both Angolan and Cuban commanders, the training of Angolan cadets in Cuba seems to have been no better. Successive commanders of the FAPA/DAA complained that the biggest part of the syllabus there was dedicated to indoctrination – especially courses in Marxism-Leninism and the history of the Cuban Revolution. Certainly enough, cadets trained in the USSR had to undergo similar indoctrination, but this was never as 'excessive' as in Cuba. Moreover, pilot training in Cuba lasted even longer: four years.[14]

Old MiGs for Mission Olivo

While the build-up of the Angolan MiG-17 squadron went exactly nowhere, that of the first MiG-21 unit of the FAPA/DAA proceeded at an even slower pace. The related affairs started moving only once Havana decided to return to fighting UNITA in a dedicated COIN-effort, Mission Olivo, in May 1981. Although this decision was certain to cause significant coordination problems, Mission Olivo operated separately from the existing MMCA chain of command, and included a flying component for which Havana requested that Moscow deliver additional MiG-21s. Overburdened with orders from elsewhere and reluctant to reinforce the campaign in Angola, the Soviets agreed to provide five old, but overhauled and slightly upgraded, MiG-21PFM fighter-bombers: unlike the MiG-21MFs, and although not suited for the task, these were deployed for COIN purposes only, in a detachment commanded by Lieutenant-Colonel Henry Peréz Martinez. These new-old MiGs arrived together with another pair of MiG-21UMs, which the MMCA used to convert a group of Angolan MiG-17 pilots to the type at Luanda IAP, during a six-month long course concluded in September 1981. However, and rather ironically considering increased tensions with South Africa, at the same time the DAA/FAR introduced the practice of sending its less-experienced pilots to Angola. Indeed, most of those arriving in Luanda as of 1981 were fresh back from conversion courses in the USSR. Certainly in order to ease just the administrative burden of the necessity to simultaneously prepare their own pilots for combat operations, and to complete the qualifications of the Angolans on the MiG-17s and MiG-21s, the Cubans concentrated all of them into their own MiG-21 unit at Lubango AB. Little better was that the Soviets simply continued monitoring the situation and did very little to help: the SMMA did not train any Angolans on MiG-21s in

A still from a video showing the MiG-21PFM C-50 of Mission Olivo while taking-off. Notably, the jet was armed with a pair of hefty ODAB-500 incendiary bombs on this occasion: although more expensive, such area-weapons proved more effective than general-purpose bombs filled with high explosive. (Albert Grandolini Collection)

1981, only three technicians in 1982, and then two pilots in 1983.[15] As should have been expected considering the state of affairs, the logical result was a series of accidents and painful mistakes – and severe losses.

Protea and other Catastrophes

On 2 May 1981, the Cuban-commanded MiG-21 unit suffered a loss in another unnecessary incident, when the MiG-21MF piloted by 1st Lieutenant Carlos Benitez Estacio was damaged by a DAA/FAR SA-3 protecting Lubango AB. The unlucky pilot attempted an emergency landing but was forced to eject and had to be recovered by helicopter. Henceforth, and in an attempt to improve the coordination between flight operations and the ground-based air defences, the HQs of the 40th BDAA and the Cuban MiG-21 unit at Lubango AB were unified into one command.[16]

In August 1981, the SADF launched Operation Protea with the aim of destroying the SWAPO command, logistics, and training centre at Xangongo, and the logistic base in Ongiva about 50 kilometres (31 miles) from the border with South West Africa. In addition to about 1,000 PLAN regulars, both Ongiva and Xangongo were protected by the FAPLA, and thus the South Africans deployed four brigade-sized task forces and supported their ground troops with massive quantities of air strikes. Indeed, taking no chances, the SAAF dedicated a large number of its sorties to the destruction of the FAPA/DAA ground-based air defences. On 23 August 1981, the

South African air force opened Operation Protea by hitting both the GAA protecting Xangongo and the one protecting Ongiva so severely that both units literally disintegrated. Two days later, the SAAF went a step further and destroyed the newly established 192nd GAAA. Another series of air strikes – flown from 27 to 29 September 1981 – knocked out the PRV-11 height-finder in Chibemba, and then repeatedly hit columns of the 185th GAAA and the 1st Radar Battalion as they marched southwards to replace the destroyed units (the 185th GAAA marched for 760 kilometres/472 miles to reach the battlefield during this campaign). Most of the attacks came so suddenly that only the 3rd Battery of the 185th – equipped with 30mm M53/59 SPAAA – managed to open fire at any of the enemy fighter-bombers.[17]

While somebody else might have given up after such a catastrophe, the experience from Operation Protea only emboldened the FAPA/DAA to further intensify its build-up. Not only did it forward-deploy the 11th and the 12th Combat Groups of the 40th BDAA, but on 6 September 1980 these claimed a SAAF 'Cessna' as shot down: reportedly, the 11th Combat Group opened this engagement with one missile, but missed, and then the 12th Combat Group fired another V-601 for a direct hit. Although direct hits by V-601 missiles were next to never scored – the missile was actually designed to detonate with a proximity fuse while approaching the target – the Angolans felt encouraged to a degree where Luanda promptly placed an order for five additional SA-3 systems (together with another 108 V-601 missiles), for delivery in 1983-1984, with the aim of establishing its third and fourth BDAAs for protection of Namibe and Matala, respectively.[18]

On the other hand, considering the immature state and preoccupation of its flying units, and their preoccupation with the necessity to train inexperienced Angolan and Cuban pilots, in is unsurprising that the FAPA/DAA failed to react to Operation Protea. MiG-21s from Lubango never rose to challenge the SAAF, and although it should have still been based at Namibe AB, the MiG-17 squadron is not known to have flown any kind of combat sorties. Indeed, the latter unit did not move even once UNITA exploited the opportunity to capture the entire Cuando Cubango province and then advance into Moxico province. Instead, it was Havana that acted by returning 2,700 specially trained COIN advisors to Angola.

First Clash with Mirages
On 6 November 1981, a pair of MiG-21MFs – both armed with four R-3S missiles and carrying a 800-litre drop tank under the centreline – launched from Lubango AB, piloted by Lieutenants Ezequiel Cancela Vázquez and Donacio Valdés Espionosa. Both fliers were junior pilots, 'pilots 3rd class' in official Cuban and Soviet jargon, still unqualified to fly combat operations. Even worse: after completing his MiG-21 conversion course in the USSR in 1979, Valdés Espinosa flew only about 38 hours over the following 16 months. Back in Cuba, he was assigned to an operational unit, and underwent his first ground attack training in January, and his basic air combat training course (though without serious manoeuvring or live firing exercises) in March and April 1981, before being ordered to Angola. However, by 6 November 1981, he clocked only 12 hours and 12 minutes of additional flight time, and never exercised in air combat or ground attack. Cancela Vázquez was appointed the leader of the pair simply because he possessed slightly more experience – about 337 hours – on the MiG-21s. Certainly enough, the task of the two pilots appeared simple: provide cover for an operation of the special forces north of the Mulando village, about 190 kilometres (118 miles) south of Lubango: essentially, that was supposed to

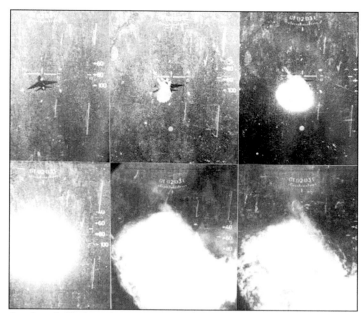

A series of stills from the gun-camera of Mirage F.1CZ flown by Major Johan Rankin showing 30mm hits on the MiG-21MF flown by Lieutenant Donacio Valdés Espinosa on 6 November 1981. The MiG was in a shallow right turn when hit: Valdés Espinosa ejected safely, shortly before his jet blew up, and was recovered. (SAAF)

be an 'uneventful mission'. However, as the MiGs approached to about 30-40 kilometres from their target zone, the ground control in Matala advised them of enemy aircraft about 120 kilometres (75 miles) away from Mulando, approaching from the south at an altitude of 4,000 metres (13,120ft) and heading for Lubango. Indeed, although knowing about the inexperience of the two MiG-21-pilots, although experiencing significant problems while trying to maintain radio contact with them, and although assuming that the enemy aircraft were Mirage F.1CZs, the tactical controller vectored them to intercept. As the four jets 'merged' – i.e. passed by within about 1,000 metres from each other – a quick dogfight ensued that was quickly concluded by the far more experienced South African Mirage F.1CZ pilots. Both Cubans were quickly outmanoeuvred: Valdés Espinosa's jet was then hit by 30mm gunfire and the pilot forced to eject, while Cancela Vázquez managed to avoid the enemy fire by a hard, descending manoeuvre, and returned safely to Lubango.[19]

Aghast at this loss, the senior leadership of the DAA/FAR ran an in-depth investigation which actually revealed nothing new: both pilots were ill-prepared for an air combat operation, and there was a communication breakdown between them and the ground control. Henceforth, the MMCA prohibited all aerial operations south of the 16th Parallel in order to avoid further encounters with the SAAF and ordered the MiG squadron in Lubango to always combine novices into formations with experienced pilots.[20]

Second Clash with Mirages
Under such circumstances, even the old MiG-17Fs flown by Angolan pilots had to be rushed into action, for example, to save the 36th BrIL when this was cut off by the FALA while underway to Cuito Cuanavale, and then to search for survivors of an Mi-8T that was shot down while carrying 19 members of the Cuban special forces, in August 1982.[21] However, the age of these jets soon began to show: in 1983, one is known to have crashed during aerobatic training over Luena, killing 2nd Lieutenant Kimo Álvaro Joâo, and another crashed on take-off from Huambo, killing Lieutenant Agostinho Sonhi. Therefore, the squadron was stood down, its

aircraft withdrawn from use, and most of its personnel sent to the USSR for another training course.[22]

Indeed, even the order to combine experienced and novice pilots made little sense because there were never enough such pilots available in Angola. This became obvious almost exactly a year later, when, on 5 October 1982, a pair of MiGs flown by Lieutenants Raciel Marrero Rodríguez (call-sign '846', on MiG-21MF C-40) and Gilberto Ortíz Pérez (call-sign '324', flying the MiG-21MF C-47) launched from Lubango to fly a combat air patrol south of the base. This time, each jet was armed with only two R-3S missiles and carried a pair of 400-litre drop tanks. Once again, both pilots were novices, lacking air combat training. Marrero Rodriguez was in the lead because with 320 hours of flight time, he was slightly more experienced. Ortíz Pérez recalled what happened during the following minutes:[23]

> The ground control ordered us up to 6,000 metres [19,685ft], and advised us about a target 10 degrees to the right, about 35 kilometres [21.7 miles] away. As we continued climbing, the next information we received was that the target was 10 kilometres [6.2 miles] away and to our right. I took a look in that direction, saw the enemy and informed my leader. The leader saw them and initiated a turn, intending to reverse behind them. I watched them pass some 300-400 metres [328-437 yards] below me and, while they were still about 10 degrees off the nose of my aircraft, I saw them ejecting their drop tanks. As we continued our turn behind them, I lost the sight of the [enemy] pair. About a minute later, I saw an enemy aircraft about 800-1,000 metres behind me in the rear-view mirror. I alerted the leader and abruptly descended to an altitude of 2,000 metres. Rolling out, I took a course of 270 degrees and began looking for the leader and the enemy but could not find them. When I turned back to base, I heard on the radio that 846 had been damaged. I had not felt any of impacts on my aircraft. When the ground control called to ask if I had any kind of problems, I answered negatively.

Actually, both MiGs were hit by gunfire from South African Mirages. Marrero Rodríguez's jet was damaged to a degree where the South Africans were convinced that they had scored their

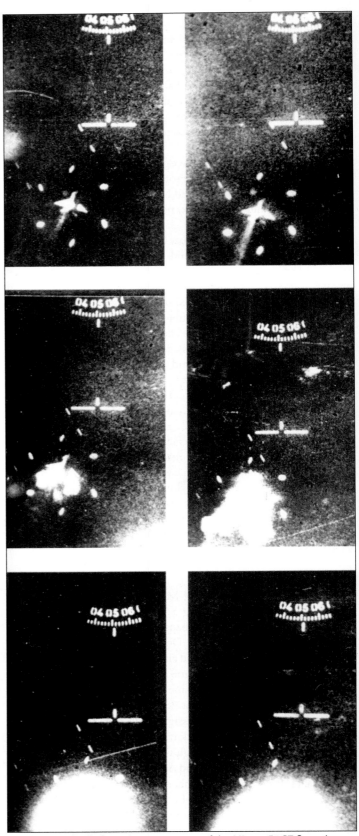

A sequence of stills from the gun-camera of the Mirage F.1CZ flown by Major Johan Rankin on 5 October 1982, showing the results of his third attack on the MiG-21MF flown by Lieutenant Kimo Álvaro Joâo: several 30mm shells hit the stabilator of the MiG, but failed to bring it down: Álvaro Joâo managed to return safely to base. (SAAF)

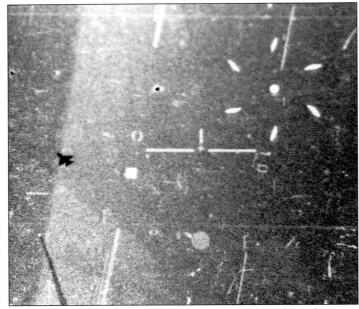

During the second air combat between DAA/FAR-operated Angolan MiG-21MFs and SAAF Mirage F.1CZs, on 5 October 1982, Major Johan Rankin fired both of the Matra R.550 Magic Mk.I air-to-air missiles installed on his aircraft. This gun camera still shows the first of the two, fired from a range of 3,000 metres, and tracking, but failing to catch the jet flown by Lieutenant Kimo Álvaro Joâo that was underway at supersonic speed. (SAAF)

The first mobile SAM system to enter service with the FAPLA was the 9K31M Strela-1 (ASCC/NATO-codename 'SA-9B Gaskin Mod1'). About 30 of these were delivered between 1975 and 1981, and they served for short-range air defence of mechanised formations. The system consisted of the hull of a BRDM-2 armoured reconnaissance car with the usual turret replaced by a mount including an optical-mechanical sighting system, atop of which were four containers with 1.8m long 9M31M infra-red homing missiles, with cooled seeker heads for improved sensitiveness. 9M31Ms had a maximum range of about 8 kilometres (5 miles) and could reach targets up to an altitude of 3,500 metres. Four such vehicles were usually combined into a single battery. In Angolan service, all the SA-9s were assigned to the motorised infantry formations of FAPLA, and usually left in dark olive green livery as on delivery. (Artwork by David Bocquelet)

During the early 1980s, FAPLA began acquiring 9K35 Strela-10 (ASCC/NATO-codename 'SA-13 Gopher') tracked SAM systems. Generally similar to the early SA-9, this system used slightly bigger 9M37 Strela-10 missiles but could also deploy a combination of these and older 9K31Ms. These were carried in containers, four of which could be installed on a pedestal atop of the MT-LB tracked chassis. However, contrary to the older SA-9, every TELAR of the SA-13 system included the 9S86, or in later sub-variants 9S16, radar rangefinder (ASCC/NATO-codenames 'Snap Shot' and 'Flat Box-B', respectively). Four TELARs were usually combined into one SAM site, but the 2nd BrIM is known to have operated a double complement with a total of eight such vehicles as of 1981-1985. As usual, all were left in dark olive green livery, as on delivery, and seem to have worn no markings at all. (Artwork by David Bocquelet)

Potentially the most threatening weapon of its kind in Angola of the mid-1980s was the 9K33M Osa-AKM/SA-8 Gecko SAM system. Moscow delivered between 12 and 15 BAZ-5937 TELARs to Angola by 1984, at least four of which were located in Cahama with the 2nd BrIM (2nd Motorised Infantry Brigade) of FAPLA. Each TEL was equipped with its own 1S51M3 'Land Roll' fire-control radar, which had three antennae: one for the main system (working in H-band) and two J-band pulse mode fire control systems. Moreover, each TEL carried six ready-to-use 9K33M missiles packed in containers that – as in the case of the SA-9 and SA-13 – also acted as launchers. As far as is known, all the Angolan SA-8 TELARs were left in dark olive green overall, as shown here. (Artwork by David Bocquelet)

In 1982, the FAPA/DAA's BN-2 unit was re-organised as the Esquadra de Reconhecimento e Assalto, and re-equipped with the first batch of Swiss-made Pilatus PC-7 light strikers. These were armed with Belgian-manufactured 90mm FN rocket pods, and usually operated in conjunction with Alouette III gunships, to search for and attack lesser insurgent camps. As far as is known, two were lost in landing accidents in 1984 (both crews uninjured), two (R-408 and R-410) collided in flight about 90km east of Luanda in mid-1985 (their crews were never found), and one to engine failure in 1986 (pilot Ruí Jesus Cardoso ejected safely and was recovered). The aircraft illustrated here belonged to the batch of attrition replacements. While at least one wore civilian livery and registration, most of the fleet was painted in the French colours Brun Café (similar to BS381C/388 Beige), Brun Noisette (similar to BS381C/350 Dark Earth) and Gris Vert Fonce (similar to BS381C/641 Dark Green) on top surfaces and sides. Undersurfaces were probably painted in Celomer 1625 Gris Bleu Moyen Clar (light blue-grey). The sole national insignia was applied in the form of a fin-flash but large black serials with the prefix R were applied on the rear fuselage. (Artwork by Tom Cooper)

After operating three Fokker F.27 transports requisitioned from civilian companies in the 1975-1976 period, the Angolans had good experiences with the type. Thus, when feeling threatened by the South African Navy and commandos, and keen to protect oilfields in the Cabinda enclave, in 1978, Luanda placed an order for two Fokker F.27-200 Maritime MPAs. Having a crew of six, the aircraft was equipped for coastal surveillance, search and rescue and environmental control missions, and capable of flying 12-hour-long patrols. However, the price tag of US$25 million per aircraft proved too much for Luanda (which could acquire a full squadron of MiG-21s for the same money). Furthermore, the FAPA/DAA was in urgent need of the highly qualified personnel necessary to operate such a complex aircraft. Thus, this remained the sole example acquired in this configuration. While originally wearing the civilian registration PH-FTU, it was re-serialled to R-301. (Artwork by Luca Canossa)

Following a major controversy in Luanda, the second F.27-200 Maritime acquired in 1978-1979 was retrograded to the F.27 Troopship configuration, and then pressed into service with the Mixed Transport Aviation Regiment wearing the serial T-101. Sadly, only black and white photographs of this aircraft are available, and thus it remains unclear what kind of camouflage colours it received: most likely, these were the same colours as used on the aircraft of the Dutch air force around the same time, including RAL 7012 grey and RAL 6014 bronze-green on upper surfaces and sides, and light grey on undersides. (Artwork by Luca Canossa)

The long-expected first jet fighter of the FAPA/DAA became the survivors of 10 MiG-17Fs and the sole MiG-15UTI originally delivered to Luanda in December 1975. While initially painted in light admiralty grey (BS381C/697) overall, by the time they were handed over to the Angolan-staffed unit that formed the core of the 26th RACB (Fighter-Bomber Regiment) in 1981, all were re-painted in beige (BS381C/388) and black-green on top surfaces and sides, while retaining light admiralty grey on undersurfaces. They were badly worn out and although easy to maintain and fly the 26th RACB lost three examples in accidents in 1983 alone. Unsurprisingly, the fleet saw very little action, was then quickly stored, and all of its personnel were sent for conversion courses to Su-20/22s. This illustration is a reconstruction of one of two examples (C23 and C24) eventually abandoned at Cuito Cuanavale airport. (Artwork by Tom Cooper)

The first batch of 12 MiG-21bis acquired by Angola was taken up by the Air Group of the DAA/FAR. They were recognisable by their big red serials in oval font, applied inconsistently in a range C61 or C62 to C99. The second and third batches consisted of MiG-21bis-Ks (recognisable by the square form of the sides of their windshields), and received serials from C301 upwards, applied in similar form. The jets in question wore the standardised camouflage pattern in beige (BS381C/388), and olive drab (BS381C/298) on top surfaces and sides, and light admiralty grey (BS381C/697) on undersurfaces. All received the large Angolan tricolore down the ruder, like Cuban-flown MiG-21MFs before them. As well as flying the mass of air strikes flown by the DAA/FAR and the FAPA/DAA in 1983 and 1984, they also stood quick alert duties, for which they were armed with much improved R-13M (ASCC/NATO-codename 'AA-2B Atoll') infra-red homing air-to-air missiles, with a limited front-aspect capability. (Artworks by Tom Cooper)

In 1984, the FAPA/DAA began receiving MiG-21bis-Ks. These wore exactly the same camouflage pattern as the jets operated by the DAA/FAR contingent, but had their serials (roughly from C321 or C322 upwards) applied in different, bigger and angular fonts. Instead of the Angolan tricolore, they wore the 'yin & yang' roundel on the fin. Contrary to the examples flown by the Cubans, the Angolan-flown MiG-21bis were almost exclusively deployed for ground attacks. Usual armament consisted of either two or four 250kg FAB-250M-54 bombs (shown here) or FAB-250M-62s, parachute-retarded OFAB-250ShNs, or UB-16-57 pods for 57mm S-5 unguided rockets. Heavier weapons were available too, including FAB-500M-62s, different variants of RBK-250 and RBK-500 cluster bomb units, and big 240mm S-24 unguided rockets – which earned themselves the nickname 'rocket bombs' – but they were rarely deployed by MiG-21s, because of their short range. (Artwork by Tom Cooper)

While the Soviets rushed 10 Su-20Ms and 2 Su-22UMs to Angola in 1983, the FAPA/DAA accepted them only a year later, when the first group of suitably trained pilots and ground personnel returned from conversion training in the USSR. The type entered service with the 26th Fighter-Bomber Aviation Regiment and was envisaged as a sort of 'silver bullet' asset: foremost expected to be used in the case of a major war with South Africa. Theoretically, Angolan Su-20Ms were to receive the same camouflage pattern as MiG-21bis delivered around the same time. However, the plant seems to have used significantly different colours instead. These included light stone (BS381C/361) and a light olive green on upper surfaces and sides, and light admiralty grey on undersurfaces. They received a standard set of serials (C501 to C510) and national markings. (Artwork by Tom Cooper)

The Su-20Ms arrived in Angola together with a shipment of relatively modern Soviet-made weapons and other equipment: indeed, some of the most advanced ever deployed in Africa at that date. Amongst the weapons were OFAB-500 pre-fragmented high-explosive bombs, shown on C501 at the top of the page. In production in the USSR since the 1970s, and in heavy demand for the war in Afghanistan, however, only relatively few reached Angola. Another advanced piece of equipment, introduced to service in the USSR in the early 1980s, is shown under C504 in this illustration: the KKR-1TE reconnaissance pod. This 6.79m long, 0.59m wide and 800kg pod contained A-39 vertical, and PA-1 and UA-47 oblique cameras. In the back was the SRS-13 Tangazh ELINT system, capable of tracking and pinpointing the work of enemy radars. They instantly converted these Sukhois into the primary reconnaissance platforms of the FAPA/DAA. Finally, for self-protection purposes, Su-20Ms were capable of carrying R-13M air-to-air missiles on inboard underwing pylons. (Artwork by Tom Cooper)

The first 12 MiG-23MLs delivered to Angola received serials C401 to C412 applied in the same fonts as the MiG-21bis-Ks operated by FAPA/DAA (and with strong inclination in line with the ground when aircraft was parked), but were all operated by the DAA/FAR contingent. Contrary to the Cuban-operated MiG-21MFs, MiG-21PFMs, and MiG-21bis, they also received the 'yin & yang' roundels in four positions: on the top of the left wing, bottom of the right wing, and on either side of the fin. As soon as declared operational, in July-August 1984, Cuban-operated MiG-23MLs took over the quick reaction alert at Lubango AB, freeing MiG-21s for fighter-bomber tasks: the latter thus flew over 400 CAS sorties during Operation FAPLA 10 Years of Victories, expending 2,700 S-5 and S-24 unguided rockets in a matter of two weeks. (Artwork by Tom Cooper)

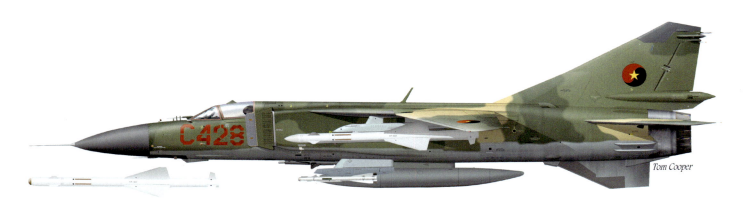

Every MiG-23ML delivered to Angola seems to have worn an entirely different camouflage pattern, frequently applied in colours that also differed from aircraft to aircraft. While C401 shown above was painted in beige (BS381C/388), dark brown (BS381C/412 or BS381C/414), and an olive shade apparently resulting from a mix of grey green (BS381C/283) and spurce green (BS381C/284), on upper surfaces and sides, and light admiralty grey (BS381C/697) on undersides, the example shown here, C428, was painted in beige (BS381C/388), green similar to the US-colour FS34151, and dark green similar to the FS34102. The undersides were usually in light admiralty grey, but some aircraft had the rear bottom of the fuselage painted in light grey instead. The standard armament of MiG-23MLs for air defence purposes consisted of one of the large R-24Rs (SARH) under the left wing, and one R-24T (infra-red homing; shown inset) under the right wing, and two R-60MKs (one installed on each of two underfuselage pylons). (Artwork by Tom Cooper)

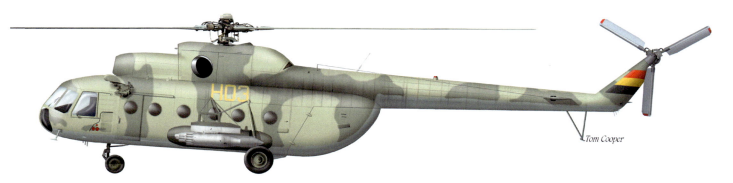

Although flying thousands of combat sorties ever since brought in by the Cubans in 1976 – the first four Mi-8Ts in Angola – serials H-01, H-02, H-03, and H-04 – remained in intensive use all through the 1980s. Apparently after receiving significant combat damage during the battle of Cangamba, in August 1983, this example was overhauled by DAA/FAR technicians at Luanda IAP and then received a new camouflage pattern in light grey-green and light olive on upper surfaces and sides, and light admiralty grey on undersides, which made it similar to Mi-8s in service in the USSR at the same time. Furthermore, this helicopter received the same hoisting winch as 12 Mi-8Ts delivered to the FAPA/DAA in 1978. Standard armament consisted of up to four UB-16-57 pods and two SPPU-6 gun-pods, of which the latter were usually installed on the centre station on either side of the helicopter. (Artwork by Tom Cooper)

While the mass of Mi-25s exported to customers in the Middle East and Africa of the late 1970s and through the 1980s were delivered wearing a camouflage pattern consisting of orange sand and green on upper surfaces and sides, Mi-25s delivered to Angola were unique in having received a camouflage pattern consisting of orange sand and chocolate brown instead. Undersurfaces were supposed to be painted in light admiralty grey, but colour photographs indicate the use of a colour with a strong touch of blue. Serials in the range H301 upwards were applied in black on the boom, and the national insignia was worn in three positions: on either side of the rear cabin, and on the bottom of the cabin. All maintenance stencils and warning insignia were in Portuguese. Primary armament consisted of UB-32-57 pods for 57mm S-5 unguided rockets. This example is illustrated as armed with AT-2 Swatter ATGMs, but these were rarely deployed in combat. (Artwork by Tom Cooper)

emerged under which the SADF's mechanised forces were to seek the destruction of enemy forces by manoeuvre, searching for, and striking weak spots, instead of a head-on clash – at operational and tactical levels. Correspondingly, South African officers of the 1980s were taught to assemble ad-hoc formations from what was available, and according to the tactical situation, into combat groups and/or combat teams, and to operate offensively. These theories were put to test in several exercises from 1973 and resulted in the creation of a permanent combined-arms unit, the 61st Mechanised Infantry Battalion, six years later. This was soon followed by additional, similar units.[1]

Counterproductive Arms Embargo

Ironically, the arms embargo imposed by the United Nations upon all sorts of arms sales to South Africa in 1979 proved entirely counterproductive: it enticed Pretoria to accelerate the development of its already bourgeoning defence industry – and was anything but universally applied. On the contrary: with a well-developed industrial base, South Africa quickly entered close cooperation with Israel and Chile, which continued unabated all through the 1980s. Results included not only the emergence of the R-4 assault rifle based on the Israeli Galil, or the development of the Atlas Aircraft Corporation Cheetah fighter-bomber, but there was close cooperation in the field of nuclear, chemical and biological weapons, too. Moreover, a network of front companies and procurement offices enabled Pretoria not only to continue importing spares and engines for SAAF Mirages from France, but also Milan ATGMs. Indeed, the South Africans went as far as to start acquiring arms from the Warsaw Pact: for example, they almost purchased 20 SA-7 grip-stocks and 160 missiles in East Germany – via Peru. However, much more important was the clandestine transfer of know-how and high technologies, which in turn were soon exported in large quantities. The direct result of all these efforts was the emergence of a vast array of locally-designed or adapted equipment, tailor-made to fit SADF doctrine. Several resulting designs – primarily mine-resistant ambush-protected (MRAP) vehicles – became benchmarks, on their own virtually dictating the world-wide evolution of similar weapons systems.[2]

Indeed, the MRAPs became the trademark of the SADF's infantry formations during the war in Angola: thousands of models named Buffel and Casspir were manufactured through the 1970s and 1980s: while lightly armoured, they provided good protection against smallarms fire. Moreover, they provided excellent protection against mines – which were planted in amazing numbers all over Angola – in turn providing motorised infantry units with high mobility. To keep such units supported, the SADF equipped itself with a fleet of Samil series trucks (including the Samil-20, Samil-50, and Samil-100). Depending on the version, these highly robust vehicles were capable of hauling 2, 5, or 10 tonnes cross-country, and had a cabin that could be armoured to protect the crew.[3]

Another entirely new design to enter service with the SADF was the Ratel (Honey Badger) infantry fighting vehicle (IFV), a unique design that was wheeled and much bigger than anything comparable, yet – despite its weight of 18,500kg – was fast, highly mobile, robust and easy to maintain. Equipped with a turret-mounted 20mm gun and a 7.62mm machine gun, it possessed considerable firepower, even if rather thin armour (the latter protected it only against bullets up to 12.7mm calibre). The Ratel in turn gave birth to an entire family of specialised vehicles, including a variant carrying an 81mm mortar, a command version, an anti-tank version (carrying the locally developed ZT-3 laser-guided ATGMs, based on the

US-made BGM-71 TOW), and the Ratel-90, which was to prove surprisingly effective in combat even against T-55M MBTs because, in addition to excellently-trained crews, most of their engagements took place in dense bush and short range, where the rapidly-turning turret of the South African IFV proved a major advantage. David Mannal, a Ratel-90 commander, later explained:

It is widely acknowledged and accepted that we had a weaker cannon and much thinner armour plate than the T-55. To survive a direct encounter our gunnery needed to be more accurate, we had to be quicker on the fire/reload cycle…and the shot had to count! A hit on a T-55's track or exposed gearing normally immobilised the platform, but the ideal strike on the seam between the hull and turret, could very well destroy the tank. In such close-quarters encounters, the 90mm HEAT [high explosive anti-tank] round proved it had sufficient power to punch through thick turret walls too, which, as it turned out, were less thick than advertised in the sales brochure we'd been shown.[…] Sometimes, it's turned, 90mm crews might've dropped the hammer four or five times before totally subduing a "T", but if a crew required so many shots they could absolutely not be firing from the same standing position. If a target was not neutralised with two shots, the crew commander had to reposition, they had to fuck with the opposite gunner. Always![4]

Meanwhile, the SADF completely overhauled its 100 outdated Centurion MBTs, and acquired additional examples from India and Jordan: with Israeli support, these were then upgraded to the model designated Olifant Mk. 1. This included reinforced armour, a new and more powerful diesel engine, and a much more potent 105mm L7 gun supported by an advanced fire-control system – all of which made it superior to whatever Soviet MBTs were operated by the Angolans and the Cubans.[5]

However, it was especially in the field of artillery where the South African defence sector proved the most successful. In 1974, a modernisation program was launched aiming to overhaul the branch, leading to the acquisition of 32 Israeli-made 120mm Soltam M5 mortars, followed by 32 155mm Soltam M71 howitzers (both were based on the designs of the Finnish company Tempella). While the M71 – re-designated to the G-4 by the SADF – proved a disappointment, it encouraged the South Africans to do more. That is how the SADF became curious about the know-how of the Space Research Corporation run by Dr. Gerald Vincent Bull, from Canada, who was working on the development of high-velocity gun designs and an entirely new generation of base-bleed shells, the so-called Extended Range Full Bore (ERFB). The Space Research Corporation had already designed the 155mm GHN-45 long-range gun, which entered production in Austria and was exported to Iraq: the company Armscor from Pretoria then acquired the licence, added a stronger mounting for increased powder loads, and installed an auxiliary power unit for improved mobility. The result was the G-5, which had a 45-calibre barrel, weighted 14 tonnes and was capable of lobbing base-bleed shells over a range of 39km (24 miles). When introduced to service in 1981, the G-5 by far the best gun of this calibre in the world, easily outmatching old 130mm M-46s of the FAPLA, which had a range of 27km (16.7 miles). Finally, during the early 1980s, the SADF introduced to service the Valkiri, a locally designed MRL-system with 24 127mm tubes installed on the reinforced and partially armoured chassis of the UNIMOG 416 truck. The shells fired by the G-5 and the rockets fired by the Valkiri could be equipped with air-burst fuses, which detonated them above the ground so to splatter shrapnel and steel balls over a much wider area than shells equipped with contact fuses. This was to prove of crucial importance for the fighting in Angola, where the typically sandy soil tended to 'gulp' most artillery ammunition, greatly dampening its effects.[6]

The only discipline in which the SADF lagged behind the FAR and the FAPLA was anti-aircraft defence. The South African Ystervark – the army's sole self-propelled anti-aircraft gun – was little more than an MRAP-like sophisticated 'technical' comprising of a 20mm gun on the chassis of the Samil-20 truck. The Swiss-made 35mm Oerlikon guns were deadly, but cumbersome, as was the French-designed R.440 Crotale radar-guided SAM. Therefore, the SADF ground forces were generally protected by Soviet-made SA-7 MANPADSs and towed ZU-23 guns – which, of course, proved insufficient: eventually, the South Africans actually depended on SAAF interceptors for air defence.[7]

SADF's Weak Spots

Overall, during the early 1980s, the SADF benefitted from an innovative doctrine, custom-tailored for the context within which it was about to operate and put into practice through suitable training of its officers and other ranks. Pretoria thus created a military machine surpassing – by far – any other armed force active in Sub-Saharan Africa: even the best units of the Cuban FAR would have been unlikely to stop a full-scale offensive into Angola including several mechanised brigades of the SADF.

Nevertheless, the South Africans all the time operated under significant constraints, which mitigated this apparent supremacy. The first was that the mass of SADF troops consisted of conscripts, all of which had spent their first year undergoing training, and then could be deployed in operational areas for only the second year of their service. This in turn meant that South African units would lose their edge whenever they had to replace the outgoing batch of conscripts and integrate a new one. As could have been expected, this regularly happened mid-way through any extended campaign. Moreover, because it was a conscript army, the SADF could ill-afford heavy casualties: this was certain to create problems with the public at home. This constraint weighted heavily on tactical and operational-level decision-making processes during virtually the entire South African involvement in the Angolan War.

Aside of this aversion to human casualties – which from time to time made high-ranking officers risk-averse – another major limitation of the SADF was its inability to go 'all-out' in Angola. While primarily related to political reasons, this issue was caused by extremely long supply lines, running all the way from South Africa via South West Africa. Although the logistical system of the SADF was to prove highly reliable and efficient, it imposed major constraints in regards of the total size of forces that could be deployed – and kept operational in the field – for any extended periods of time, even more so because the last leg of this supply chain was within an area almost completely devoid of good roads. For example, while a total of 2,268 kilometres of roads connected Pretoria with Grootfontein, it took five days of road travel to cross just 356 kilometres from Rundu, on the Angolan border, to Mavinga. In this regard, even the SAAF could not help sufficiently, due to the small size of its transport fleet, and the lack of adequate airports within UNITA-controlled Angola. Indeed, the main available hub, the 'airfield' of Mavinga, was little more than a strip cleared in the bush, always exposed to enemy air strikes.[8]

TABLE 7: Known FALA Battalions	
Number	Comments
1	regular, est. 1985
2	regular, est. 1985
3	regular, est. 1985
4	regular, existent in 1987
5	regular, existent in 1987
7	semi-regular, existent in 1983
8	regular as of 1989
9	semi-regular, existent in 1989
12	semi-regular, existent in 1989
14	semi-regular, existent in 1983
15	semi-regular, existent in 1985
17	semi-regular, existent in 1983
18	semi-regular, existent in 1985
22	semi-regular, existent in 1983
24	semi-regular, existent in 1983
26	semi-regular, existent in 1983
49	semi-regular, existent in 1985
54	semi-regular, existent in 1989
65	semi-regular
66	semi-regular, existent in 1983
75	semi-regular, existent in 1989
85	semi-regular existent in 1987
89	semi-regular, all-female unit, existent in 1989
90	semi-regular, existent in 1983
111	semi-regular, existent in 1983
117	semi-regular, existent in 1983
118	semi-regular, existent in 1985
154	semi-regular, existent in 1985
179	semi-regular, existent in 1985
210	semi-regular, existent in 1981
275	semi-regular, existent in 1981
327	semi-regular, existent in 1980
333	semi-regular, existent in 1983
360	semi-regular, existent in 1981
369	semi-regular, existent in 1983
415	semi-regular, existent in 1983
423	semi-regular, existent in 1983
513	semi-regular, existent in 1986
517	semi-regular, existent in 1983
618	semi-regular, existent in 1983

Growing UNITA

In turn, and with hindsight, it is notable that the Angolans – and their Cuban and Soviet supporters – never found a way to exploit all the opportunities offering themselves to at least temporarily disturb, if not seriously disrupt, the SADF's major operations into Angola during the 1980s. Nowhere was this as obvious as in the continuous growth of UNITA and its military wing, FALA.

Of Strelas and Stingers

The FALA received its first MANPADs in the form of a batch of SA-7s as early as 1976. They were delivered by the CIA, which acquired them from Israel. Indeed, the Americans went as far as to provide a team of French mercenaries trained to use the Soviet-made MANPADS, via Zaire. Certainly enough, both missiles and their operators failed to leave any lasting impressions against the Cuban-operated MiGs in that year: all the SA-7s that were fired missed their targets. The apparent reason was that the Israelis had delivered these in poor condition; however, Savimbi also hinted that the French mercenaries proved unable to deploy them effectively.

In late 1979 and early 1980, UNITA acquired another batch of 200 SA-7s from the External Documentation and Counter-Espionage Service (Service de Documentation Extérieure et de Contre-Espionage, SDECE), of France: these were used by FALA to claim an An-26 shot down on 19 October 1980 as it was bombing an airstrip outside Luenge, and a TAAG An-26 on take-off from Mpupa airport (the latter was operated by Aeroflot, and its shoot-down resulted in the insurgents capturing two of its Soviet crew-members, Mollaeb Kolya, and Ivan Chernietsk).[11]

During Operation Protea, in 1981, the SADF captured extensive stocks of SA-7s, and nearly all of these found their way into the FALA's arsenals, ensuring that the insurgency could threaten DAA/FAR and FAPA/DAA aircraft for years in advance. Moreover, the French – who were known to have been acquiring SA-7s from Egypt and Czechoslovakia – then provided additional examples through the so-called 'Safari Club'.[12]

However, the SA-7 was a 1st generation MANPAD, quite limited in its capabilities and reach. Its primary weakness was that the operator requiring forewarning and time to power-up the system before engaging. Hence, the SA-7 was rarely successful in practice, unless engaging low and slow-flying targets. The situation was to change only in mid-1985, when the US Congress abolished the Clark Amendment (which prohibited provision of support for any kind of insurgency in Angola), and the administration of US President Ronald Reagan then decided to provide 'non-lethal military' equipment worth US$15 million to UNITA. The first batch of 50 FIM-92A Stinger MANPADs was to reach Jamba in early 1986. It was followed by many more over the next two years, as the Reagan administration almost doubled its aid. By 1989, the FALA is known to have received 310 Stingers. Although frequently claimed a such, the FIM-92A was no 'cure-all' or a 'wonder weapon', but its introduction into service by well-versed FALA units was to have major, and direct impacts upon the air war – not only because of the number of aircraft shot down by it, but because it forced Angolan and Cuban pilots into a drastic change of their tactics, with the aim of limiting their exposure to the Stinger. This in turn had negative impacts upon the precision of their air strikes.[13]

Regardless if equipped with Strelas or with Stingers, the FALA units operating MANPADs were small anti-aircraft batteries (baterias móveis), overall commander of which was Colonel Jõao Cristiano 'Susula'. They were assigned either to conventional or to guerrilla units as necessary, and frequently underway next to enemy air bases and airfields, or below known aerial corridors.[14]

Members of one of FALA's 'anti-aircraft batteries' preparing one of their two SA-7 MANPADs for action. (Tom Long Collection)

An SA-7 captured during Operation Protea, in the hands of a South African soldier. (Albert Grandolini Collection)

On the contrary, through the early 1980s, the provision of South African support grew to such an extent that it enabled an almost undisrupted growth of the insurgency. By 1984, the Strategic Operational Command (Comando Operacional Estratégico, COPE) of the FALA comprised five fronts and 23 military regions active almost everywhere around Angola, even if mostly limited to typical guerrilla operations such as hit-and run attacks, minelaying, and ambushes. By 1987, the movement claimed to have up to 65,000 combatants, of which around 37,000 were part-time militia and guerrilleros, usually organised into detachments of around 150 men. The other 28,000 were organised into what the FALA termed 'strategic forces': organised into semi-regular battalions, these were trained to conduct semi-conventional, or even conventional, operations of large scale, and were never active either within so-called 'UNITA-controlled areas', nor within 'contested areas'. By 1987, the FALA included at least 40 such units – each anywhere between 250 and 650 strong – and continued establishing them at an average rate of four per annum. Each FALA battalion consisted of several infantry companies and one support company. Infantry companies were relatively lightly armed: as well as a wide range of assault rifles, they had a few medium machine guns, RPG-7s, and 60mm mortars. For the conduct of large-scale operations multiple battalions were assigned to brigade headquarters. However, when not only the Cubans returned to COIN warfare, but FAPLA began growing in sophistication, it became progressively obvious that even more powerful units would be necessary. Correspondingly, starting in 1985, the FALA began establishing regular battalions: these included at last 800 officers and other ranks with extensive training, and comprised powerful support elements, including mortar platoons with eight 81mm tubes. Two years later, at least five such units were existent, designated 1-5, while another four followed by 1989.[9]

Meanwhile, the FALA established an artillery battalion (pooling all the captured heavy armament into a motley collection of batteries equipped with ZiS-3 guns, 120mm mortars, 106mm recoilless rifles, and Type-63 MRLs), one anti-aircraft unit (equipped with light AAA and MANPADs), and a unit operating a few T-34/85 tanks and other captured armoured vehicles. Finally, starting in 1987, the FALA units were equipped with French-made APILAS anti-tank rockets and then US-provided BGM-71 TOW ATGMs.

In addition to this range of guerrilla and conventional units, the FALA began building up a number of smaller, 'elite' units. Foremost amongst these were penetration battalions – units specialised in long-range raids deep behind enemy lines – eight of which were established by 1989. Perhaps the most famous became the Brigade for Deployment of Explosive Charges (Brigada de Accao de Tecnica de Explosivos): established in the early 1980s, and commanded by Brigadier George Niolela Diamantino, this was a special forces unit trained to carry out long-range reconnaissance, organised into 16 groups of 50 fighters each (each group included four sections of 10 troops, a headquarters and a support section). Finally, the FALA had specialised units, including engineer, reconnaissance and commando platoons, deployed to support other forces as necessary.

Such a large structure required a corresponding training system. The primary training facility was the Commandante Monteira Training Camp in the Jamba area: supported by a number of South African instructors, this had an annual output of about 8,000. Further, smaller camps were constructed to provide advanced and specialised training, and there was a separate facility for officer training: unsurprisingly, UNITA produced a number of gifted commanders, like General Arlindo Chenda Pena 'Big Ben', General Bok Sepalalo and General Demóstenos Amós Chilingutila, to name a few. In this way, and even if remaining unable to stop major FAPLA offensives, the FALA gradually developed into a well-disciplined and well-organised, light infantry force with high striking power.[10]

6

Bitter 1983

Considering the reinforced South African support for UNITA, Pretoria's preparedness to run externals into Angola and especially the SMMA and FAPLA's ignorance of the necessity to confront the insurgency with full force, the next catastrophe for Angola was inevitable. Through the first half of 1983, the FALA forced the evacuation of several isolated FAPLA garrisons from the Cuando-Cubango province. Emboldened, the insurgents then launched preparations for a massive blow against Cangamba, a small town in southern Moxico province. Thus began only the first taste of what – for the FAPLA – was to become the bitter experience of 1983.

Cangamba Shock

Situated roughly halfway between the towns of Kuito and Luena on the Benguela Railway, and Cuito Cuanavale, Cangamba was controlled by exhausted and depleted command and support elements of the 32nd BrIL and one of that brigade's infantry battalions, a weak company from the 44th BrIL, and 92 Cuban advisors. Moreover, its defence perimeter consisted of partially unprotected minefields, and a trench-line lacking communication links and fortifications. Only the inside perimeter – including the HQ of the 32nd BrIL and the Cuban contingent – was better defended. For this operation, UNITA's military wing, the FALA, amassed over 3,000 combatants from four of its semi-regular battalions, supported by 60mm, 81mm, and 120mm mortars, a few captured 76mm ZiS-3 field guns, several SA-7 teams, and seven 14.5mm ZPU-4 quadruple machine guns. Finally, the South Africans provided extensive support in the form of ammunition and supplies deployed in nocturnal flights by SAAF transport aircraft.

The onslaught began at dawn of 2 August 1983, with a heavy artillery barrage – which, amongst other things, badly damaged the DAA/FAR An-26 T-202, piloted by Avelino Passos Costa, forcing the crew to abandon the aircraft in situ – followed by a multipronged infantry assault around noon. Initially, the FALA managed to punch through the outside perimeter and enter the eastern side of the town. However, the garrison held out and called for help. By early afternoon, three MiG-21PFMs (including C-55 and C-111, flown by Henry Pérez Martinez, Edilberto Lee King, and Rigoberto Riverón) of Mision Olivo were re-deployed via Huambo to Menongue, from where they flew the first two close-air support (CAS) attacks. During the afternoon, four additional MiG-21bis – flown by Oscar Romero, Raúl Fernandez, Gustavo Alonso, and Ramón Quesada) – arrived in Menongue, followed by a pair of MiG-21MFs (piloted by Jorge Lombidez and Fidel Pérez). The aircraft were quickly turned around, loaded with UB-16-57 pods and RBK-250 bombs, and sent into another attack, led by Pérez and Lee King in MiG-21PFMs. These 11 air strikes devastated the FALA infantry, forcing it to withdraw. Although realising that their plot had failed, UNITA commanders decided to continue this operation and rushed in reinforcements in the form of three additional battalions. Since it took time for these to arrive, between 3 and 5 August the fighting for Cangamba became an ugly battle of attrition. On 3 August, the nine DAA/FAR pilots available at Menongue flew 21 strike missions; operating from Luena, a FAPA/DAA An-26 bomber flew two additional bombing sorties. Furthermore, a day later the MiGs provided cover for four Mi-8s that brought in an urgently needed doctor, and Julio Chiong – a grounded Cuban pilot equipped

A formation of Mi-8Ts of the DAA/FAR underway at low altitude armed with UB-16-57 pods and SPPU-6 gun pods for 23mm cannons (centre hardpoint). Just four helicopters of this type operated by Cuban pilots played a decisive role by flying air strikes, bringing reinforcements and supplies to and evacuating casualties from the besieged garrison of Cangamba in August 1983. (Verde Olivo)

with a radio, who was to act as a forward air controller (FAC) – while evacuating casualties. The insurgent anti-aircraft fire was fierce, but, although causing damage to several MiGs and all of the helicopters, it failed to bring down any of the aircraft. Moreover, the FALA – resupplied by nocturnal drops by SAAF transports – continued pushing and by 5 August the garrison was forced to withdraw to the inner defence perimeter. One of the reasons was that from that day onwards, South African interceptors flew regular demonstration sorties well within the range of FAPA/DAA's radars in Menongue: their presence could not be ignored, and thus the Cuban

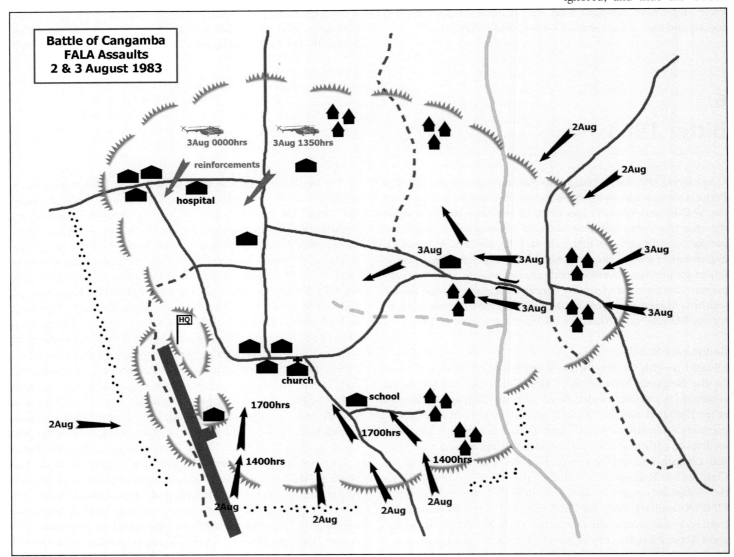

A map of the Battle of Cangamba, showing FALA's assaults from 2 August (south and north-east) and from 3 August (east). At the highest point, the insurgents controlled nearly half of the perimeter. However, reinforcements inserted by Mi-8 helicopters into the north-western corner on two occasions, and a series of vicious air strikes turned the tables. From Cuban accounts, Mission Olivo's pilots primarily targeted the eastern part of the perimeter, but also the local church, school, and the southern side of the airport. (Map by Tom Cooper)

An aerial view of Cangamba as of 1983, as seen from the eastern side. (Verde Olivo)

MiG pilots were forced into escorting every air strike against UNITA at Cangamba with at least two MiG-21bis armed with air-to-air missiles. This in turn reduced the amount of ordnance they could unleash upon the enemy. Moreover, the MiGs operated so intensively, that they rapidly exhausted the DAA/FAR and FAPA/DAA ammunition dumps on nearby bases. By 7 August, the USSR and Cuba had to launch an air bridge involving one Il-62 flight from Havana to Luanda, and 40 An-26s, 28 An-12s, 21 C-130 and 6 Boeing 707 flights inside Angola to bring in 16,000 litres of aviation fuel, 400 bombs, 3,000 23mm rounds, and almost 4,000 S-5K rockets to airfields in Menongue and Luena. Finally, the FAR rushed its elite Airborne Brigade to Angola, where it arrived on 11 August, while between 18 and 23 August, three merchant ships hauled an entire armoured brigade in the same direction.[1]

On 10 August, UNITA gave up and issued the order for FALA to withdraw. For all practical purpose, the battle was a clear-cut victory for the MMCA and the FAPLA. However, at that point in time Castro – convinced that despite the defensive success, and because of the approaching rain season the garrison was still much too exposed – issued an order for withdrawal of the Cuban contingent from Cangamba: this was flown out by Mi-8s two days later. On the contrary, certain that the place would be an excellent springboard for a counteroffensive, the commander of the SMMA, Colonel-General Konstantin Kurochkin, convinced the MPLA and the FAPLA to stay. Meanwhile, Savimbi did his best to convince the South Africans to become involved and surprisingly enough Pretoria agreed. On 14 August 1983, eight fighter-bombers of the SAAF flew a devastating air strike, after which even the Angolans gave up: the FAPLA garrison of Cangamba was withdrawn to Tempue the following day. In their wake, the insurgents were free to claim a massive victory because they were now in control of the battlefield.

Nunda's Cavalcade

Despite losses suffered by the FALA in Cangamba, its 10 battalion strong Northern Front – commanded by Brigadier Geraldo Nunda – launched another offensive only a month later, when it blew up the 200-metre long Cuango Bridge on the road connecting Saurimo and Luena, and then besieged the town of Cuemba, on the Benguela railway. The Cubans reacted with additional air strikes, and these forced the insurgents to withdraw, but thanks to South African

supplies, UNITA was quick to recover. On 13 November 1983, a large FALA force overran the garrison of Cazombo, capturing vast stocks of weapons and ammunition, and 36 foreigners (including 34 Portuguese and 2 Canadian nuns). With this, a 150-kilometre-long stretch of the border between Angola and Zambia was under insurgent control, and even Luena was essentially cut off from the outside world. When FAPLA failed to react, Brigadier Nuna invested the garrison of Andulo on 26 November 1983, followed, three days later, by Alta Chiapa: while Andulo held out, the FAPLA garrison in Alta Chiapa broke down and ran away. Having his battalions partially grouped into a brigade, and reinforced by some armour the South Africans had captured during Operation Protea in 1981, Nuna then moved his units 100 kilometres further north: on 18 December, he overran the garrison of Cacolo. A month later, on 24 January 1984, he returned to assault Nova Sintra on the Benguela Railwway, and on 23 February Cafunfo – including the local mining facility that was the source of about a third of the diamonds exported by Angola at the time: 106 foreigners captured there – including four British guards (all ex-Special Air Service operators, hired to provide security) – were taken away.

Once again, there was no reaction from the MMCA and the FAPLA: the two were preoccupied running their own counteroffensive, further south – and that was the kind of enterprise that always proceeded at a very slow pace. From 5 September until 24 October 1983, the mass of units of Military Regions 4, 7, and 9 of the FAPLA, reinforced by the MMCA's Tactical Group Quibala, the Spear of the Nation Battalion of the African National Congress (ANC), and one of two motorised brigades of the PLAN, ran Operation MPLA's 27th Anniversary to recapture the towns of Calulo and Mussende. This operation was supported by a massive volume of sustained air strikes: the DAA/FAR and the FAPA/DAA flew 1,004 combat and 160 reconnaissance sorties, and the insurgents admitted suffering 82 killed. In turn, on 20 October 1983, they shot down the MiG-21PFM C-54 flown by the commander of Mission Olivo, Lieutenant-Colonel Henry Pérez Martinez. Moreover, on 8 November 1983, a FAPA SA-7 Team Grupo de BATE infiltrated the outskirts of Lubango to set up an ambush and shot down a Boeing 737 airliner belonging to TAAG, killing all 130 of the crew and passengers aboard.[2]

South Africa's Next External[3]

Meanwhile, through early and mid-1983, the SADF had concluded that PLAN was in the process of preparing a large-scale infiltration campaign of South West Africa during the forthcoming rainy season. Correspondingly, a decision was taken to pre-empt that effort through launching an offensive into the Cunene province of Angola and destroying as much of the insurgent infrastructure as possible. However, contrary to the situation from 1981, two years later the PLAN bases in northern Cunene could rely on a network of FAPLA garrisons to shield them: this meant that the SADF would have to attack and destroy regular Angolan armed forces in order to meet its objective. Of course, such an effort would offer an incentive in so far that landing crippling blows upon the FAPLA would relieve pressure upon UNITA.

Considering the above-mentioned list of aims, it is unsurprising that the SADF eventually prepared for a large-scale operation. Codenamed Operation Askari, this envisaged the deployment of five combined-arms task forces led by Brigadier Joep Joubert:

- Task Force X-Ray: 61st Mechanised Battalion, including three mechanised infantry companies mounted on Ratel-20s, and one squadron of Ratel-90s, two troops of Valkiri MRLS, two artillery batteries (one with eight 155mm G-4 guns, and one with eight 140mm G-2 guns), and two anti-aircraft batteries with 20mm guns. The main objectives of Task Force X-Ray were Quiteve and Cahama.
- Task Force Victor: two mechanised companies of the Citizen Force units mounted on Ratel-20s, one Eland-90 squadron, a single G-2 battery, one Valkiri troop and two 20mm anti-aircraft troops. The main objective was Cuvelai.
- Task Force Echo Victor: 32nd Buffalo Battalion, which was to isolate PLAN camps and bases in the northern Cuvelai from the local FAPLA garrisons.
- Combat Team Tango: one mechanised infantry company mounted on Buffels, one Eland-90 squadron, and one troop of G-2 guns.
- Combat Team Manie: two infantry companies drawn from 202nd Battalion and 7th South African Infantry Regiment, one Eland-90 squadron, and one platoon of 81mm mortars. Its primary objective was deception: this formation was to simulate the existence of a third main advance by harassing FAPLA garrisons in the Caiundo area.

For the support of Operation Askari, the SAAF mobilised four Canberra and four Buccaneer bombers, ten Impala II light strikers, and ten Alouette helicopters, while additional units were on standby and ready for a quick deployment should the need arise.

FAPLA's Regulars

Notably, the plan for Operation Askari envisaged no direct attacks by ground units upon PLAN camps: instead, the SADF aimed to isolate its objectives – especially from nearby FAPLA garrisons – and then harass them with artillery and mortars and also by air strikes, until the insurgents would be compelled to withdraw on their own. Dubbed 'uitmergeling' – 'squeezing dry' – these tactics meant that the success of the entire enterprise depended on the ability of the SADF to break the will to fight of the FAPLA. Unsurprisingly, the original plan for Operation Askari expected this to last for about two months. However, while the planning and preparations for Operation Askari proceeded well, the enterprise had to be postponed several times, primarily because of the growing international pressure upon Pretoria. Thus, the offensive was unleashed only in December 1983, during the rainy season: this resulted in a considerably slower movement of mechanised forces than originally planned – and that was only the first problem encountered. Another issue emerged once the battle was joined and was related to the massive underestimation of the opposition.

Lieutenant-Colonel Henry Peréz Martinez, commander of Mission Olivo, was the pilot of the MiG-21PFM C-54 when the latter was hit by FALA ground fire on 20 October 1983. Peréz Martinez attempted to fly the badly damaged jet back to Luena but was eventually forced to make a belly landing. (Still from TV-documentary Operation Carlota)

As of late 1983, within the area of Operation Askari, and from west to east, FAPLA had the following units:

- 2nd BrIM, deployed in Cahama and Ediva
- 19th BrI, in Mulando
- 11th BrI, in Cuvelai
- 53rd BrIL, in Caiundo.

Except for the 53rd BrIL – a light infantry formation with slightly less than 1,000 officers and other ranks protecting Caiundo and subordinated to the 6th Military Region – all of these units were controlled by the HQ of the 5th Military Region and maintained at full strength. Thus, they counted

Wreckage of Mission Olivo's MiG-21PFM C-54 as found by FALA insurgents, after its belly landing outside Luena. By the time of their arrival, the aircraft was already destroyed and Peréz Martinez had been recovered by helicopter. (Photo by Al J Venter)

A Venomous Gecko

During the traditional May Day parade in Red Square in Moscow on 1 May 1976, the USSR surprised the Western observers by presenting a brand-new, highly mobile air defence system. Designated 9K33 Osa, this consisted of the elements listed in Table 8. Its most remarkable components were four big, six-wheeled BAZ-5937 self-propelled transporter-erector-launchers with radar (TELARs), each originally carrying four 9K33 surface-to-air missiles. Although each of the four TELARs was equipped with a large, one-man gunner-radar operator mount with an early warning radar (ASCC/NATO-codename 'Land Roll'), and its own fire-control radar, and thus capable of operating on its own, the actual centrepiece of every SA-8 SAM site was the 9A33B mobile early warning radar, and a radar collimation vehicle, which exercised control over its operations. Each TELAR had a crew of four that, on average, required between three and six months of training to become fully operational: these were three radar operators (one for the search radar, one for the guidance of the missile, and one for determining the target range), and the driver. A SAM site of four TELARs included additional personnel, the most important of who were communication technicians: they were responsible for maintaining links between individual TELs. Under ideal conditions, the Land Roll early-warning/fire-control system had a range of about 30km, enabling a lock-on at a range of about 20km, and the missile to engage targets out to a range of about 15km.

Angola acquired the slightly upgraded 9K33M Osa-AKM (SA-8b Gecko), the TELARs of which were equipped to carry up to six 3.15m long, radio-command-guided 9K33M missiles, all packed and sealed inside their own transport containers which also acted as 'launch rails'. Each container included a link that could be coupled to a test-rig from which the crew could check the state of the missile before deploying it. Moreover, the Osa-AKM arrived equipped with an optical tracker based on low-light TV-technology, enabling it to operate in 'optical mode', despite heavy electronic countermeasures: in other words, the Osa was able to operate without any kind of radar support, and thus without alerting enemy pilots of its presence – through radar emissions intercepted by radar-warning receivers (RWRs) installed into SAAF Mirages, for example.

Contrary to what might be expected, the Angolan and Cuban SA-8 operators in Angola did not power up their Land Roll radars all the time: on the contrary, they would activate them only when operationally necessary, and

then for several minutes at most. The reason was that in this fashion the SA-8 SAM site could conceal its position from South African electronic reconnaissance (ELINT). Nevertheless, in action, the system proved most effective if supported by the Land Roll. In turn, the function of the radar depended on the operationality of its radiofrequency generator ('HF-generator') – which proved to be the weakest part of the entire system. Each of the four TELs was equipped with one HF-generator: based on analogue, vacuum-tube technology, this had an average service life of about 700 hours, and was a unique piece of equipment that could be sourced from the USSR only. The HF-generator supporting the work of the Land Roll radar took between three and five minutes to warm up and enable the radar operation – which was a relatively long time in aerial warfare. Once the HF-generator was powered up, the radar operator required 'only' to push a single button for the radar to start transmitting. However, then it took time to scan the area around the SAM site, detect a target, distinguish it from ground clutter, identify it as a friend or foe, lock-on and only then was the system ready to fire. Both the radar and the HF-generator tended to suffer a lot when operated for short periods.

Almost immediately on its arrival in Angola in 1983, the SA-8 proved a major hindrance for the South Africans, who lacked not only reliable intelligence on the system, but also had no means of electronic countermeasures (ECM) against it.

Table 8: Major Equipment of standard SA-8b SAM Site

Equipment and Observations	Number per site
9A33BM mobile EW-radar	1
Radar collimation vehicle	1
BAZ-5937 6x6 TELAR	4
9T217 transloader vehicles	2

A typical TELAR of the SA-8 system. (Al J Venter Collection)

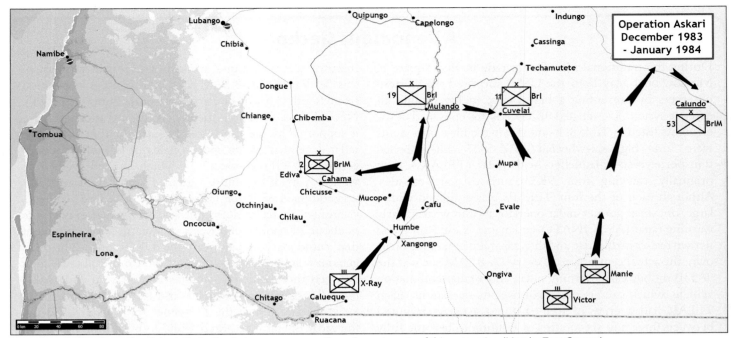

Map of the SADF's Operation Askari. Underlined place names were the primary targets of this enterprise. (Map by Tom Cooper)

about 6,000 officers and other ranks, and each brigade HQ had a group of 12-14 Soviet instructors assigned. Furthermore, the 11th BrI and the 19th BrI were equipped with T-55 MBTs armed with a 100mm D-10T gun, which was to prove vastly superior to the 90mm low-velocity guns of Eland-90s and Ratel-90s of the SADF. Their artillery complements were also significantly stronger than at earlier times: the 2nd BrIM, 11th BrI and the 19th BrI each had a battery of 122mm D-30 howitzers that outranged South African G-2s, and the 2nd BrIM included at least a battery of even longer-ranged 130mm M-46 cannons. All these three major units had constructed elaborate and formidable systems of well-concealed fortifications: indeed, aside of extensive minefields, trench systems, and bunkers, their defensive perimeters were surrounded by clear fields of fire, where all trees and the bush had been cut, and often converted into (usually: one metre tall) obstacles for vehicles, camouflaged by maize. Moreover, regular troops from these units underwent improved training and ran intensive patrols as far as 20 kilometres in front of their main positions, while their organic armour elements were prepared to react in a much more aggressive fashion than ever before – instead of sitting and waiting as static pillboxes. The command of the 2nd BrIM was especially adept at quickly shifting elements of that brigade from one point to another, whenever the actual axis of the enemy attack was detected, while its air defence units were constantly rotated around the brigade.[4]

The latter issue was of particular importance because, in the light of previous experiences with the murderous effectiveness of SAAF air strikes, all of these units were reinforced by a host of anti-aircraft assets of the FAPA/DAA. For example, Cahama was additionally protected by the entire 192nd GAAA, which now included one battery each of 30mm and 37mm guns. Moreover, the 2nd BrIM included the first Soviet-made 9K33 Osa (ASCC/NATO-codename 'SA-8 Gecko') mobile SAM system delivered to Angola. Once again, it was only the 53rd BrIL that was to prove to have been left virtually defenceless: this unit operated only ZPU-1 heavy machine guns and SA-7s.

Askari derailed

Operation Askari began during November 1983, with the infiltration of several teams of the Reconnaissance Regiment, SADF, into the areas around Cahama, Mulondo, Cuvelai, and Lubango, with the aim of finding and assessing enemy positions. Crucially, one of the teams was detected and involved in a brief exchange of fire with a group of PLAN insurgents: this proved enough for SWAPO to activate its own contingency planning for the event of an imminent South African offensive, and evacuate most of its bases. On the contrary, the SADF was left with no choice but to go on as planned.

On the western-most axis, Task Force X-Ray reached Quiteve on 12 December 1983, only to find out that the garrison had already evacuated – even though leaving behind large stocks of supplies. The 19th BrI reacted by detaching an infantry force supported by two T-55s, but this was forced back after being exposed to SAAF air strikes, losing one tank in the process. The bulk of Task Force X-Ray then turned west and went straight for the 2nd BrIM's stronghold in Cahama, while another combat group continued north, to harass the 19th BrI in Mulando. Indeed, as planned, the latter place was then exposed to a series of artillery and air strikes: however, these proved far less effective than expected. On the contrary, the D-30 howitzers of the 19th BrI proved superior to the South African G-2s, especially when deployed with support of well-concealed forward artillery observers: in other words, the SADF artillery encountered precise counter-battery fire, whenever attempting to join the battle, forcing gunners to move often, and thus reducing the number of shells it was able to lob at Mulando. To make matters even more problematic, the presence of the SA-8 SAM system made it impossible for the SAAF to use light aircraft as forward artillery observers: instead, SADF artillery had to make use of much less precise sound direction-finding systems, and the few Israeli-made Seeker unmanned aerial vehicles (UAVs) that were now on hand. With the later still essentially prototypes and available only in limited numbers, this was far from satisfactory. Finally, Angolan air defences proved more effective than expected: this became obvious on 23 December, when one of two Impalas deployed to attack Mulando with 68mm unguided rockets was hit by an SA-7. While its pilot, Lieutenant Neels Meintjes managed to nurse the crippled jet to

A row of Impala Mk.IIs: this light striker was based on the design of the Aeromacchi MB.326, but equipped with only one cockpit and manufactured under licence by Atlas in South Africa. It formed the backbone of the SAAF during the early 1980s and flew the highest number of combat sorties during Operation Askari. (SAAF)

a safe landing at Ondangwa Forward Operating Base (FOB), the message was clear: the Angolans were ready and alert.[5]

South African experiences in the Cahama area were exactly the same. Task Force X-Ray's G-4 battery began an engage the 2nd BrIM, but the commander of the latter reacted by deploying a company of T-55s into a counterattack on 14 December. The Angolan armour nearly reached the South African artillery before, only three kilometres short of its precious target, it ran into the elements of the 61st Mechanised Battalion, acting as goalkeeper. While the Angolan T-55s were stopped, the South African artillerists were left with no choice but to withdraw as fast as they could – and even then their convoy was bracketed by a volley of an entire BM-21 battery, before the latter was silenced by SAAF Impalas. What actually saved the day for the SADF was the fact that the 122mm Grad rockets of the BM-21 battery in question were all equipped with delay-fuses: thus, they penetrated deep into the ground before detonating, greatly reducing their lethal range.[6]

Ultimately, the more manoeuvrable SADF might have gained the upper hand during continuous artillery duels, if it was not for the SA-8 SAM site of the 2nd BrIM, which damaged one of the Seeker UAVs with a volley of three 9K33M missiles. Because the Seekers were still a scarce asset, they were immediately withdrawn from the combat zone, leaving the G-4s without their most effective targeting device.

On 20 December 1983, a team from Task Force X-Ray finally found a gap in the FAPLA lines, outflanked the Cahama complex and dashed for Chibemba in a simulated advance for Lubango – a neuralgic spot on the eastern side of the Fidel Castro Line. FAPLA promptly reacted by deploying a column of T-55s and BTRs from Chibemba: this found the South Africans and – in a short clash – forced their combat team to withdraw, thus calling off the bluff. Two days later, on 22 December 1983, gunners operating M-46s of the 2nd BrIM had a particularly successful day: they hit the G-4 battery, destroying one of its gun tractors and wounding two crew, before rattling positions of the 61st Mechanised Battalion and destroying a Ratel-20. Finally, on 23 December 1983, a feinted SADF attack towards Cahama was easily repulsed by the Angolans, making it obvious that the 'uitmergeling' tactic was not working against the best of FAPLA.[7]

Although Operation Askari was thus completely derailed, the South Africans continued to engage for a few days longer. In the Cuvelai area, Task Force Victor probed the 11th BrI, mainly with the help of its G-2 guns, which triggered a number of exchanges. However, on at least one occasion the Angolan D-30 gunners bracketed the position of their counterparts, destroying another gun tractor and a truck, even if without inflicting casualties. The "dot on the i" was provided by the 11th BrI on 23 December 1983, when its elements took the South Africans by surprise through moving out in the direction of Task Force Victor: the SADF was forced to redirect another of its task forces in this direction, in order to effect a safe withdrawal.[8]

Perhaps the most unpleasant surprise of Operation Askari was experienced by the lightly-equipped Combat Team Manie, which was supposed to run a diversion by harassing Caiundo. Indeed, the also lightly-equipped 53rd BrIL, actually a COIN asset without any heavy armour or artillery bar a few mortars and Grad-1P single tube rocket launchers, proved as aggressive as the 2nd BrIM. The Angolan patrols detected the approach of a composite platoon from the 202nd Battalion SADF on 17 December, as this was camping about 12 kilometres outside Caiundo. The next night, the HQ of 53rd BrIL deployed an infantry company to attack, masked by a mortar barrage. The Angolans attacked the next dawn, taking the South Africans completely by surprise, killing eight and capturing one. The SADF left behind four Buffels (including one intact), four light machine guns, 14 R1 assault rifles, four radios, three RPG-7s, one US-made M79 grenade launcher, and a single 60mm mortar. The pursuers were stopped only when targeted by SAAF fighter-bombers.

This experience instantly converted Caiundo into a new major target for the South Africans and the SAAF – until then not even aware of the presence of SADF ground troops in that area – found itself ordered to divert from its main efforts against Cahama, Cuvelai, and Malundo, and fly air strikes there. Furthermore, Combat Team Manie was reinforced through the addition of one company from the 32nd Battalion, one parachute company, one detachment of Eland armoured cars, and a team with four 120mm mortars. Unsurprisingly, it was renamed Combat Group Delta Foxtrot and received a new commander: Colonel Deon Ferreira. Bolstered, the with Kurochkin:

> Our forces are growing and the talks could be started in more appropriate conditions. It would be much more advantageous to conduct negotiations in a year or a year and a half's time: we would have MiG-23s, Kvadrats and a much stronger air defence. The talks should have been interrupted as soon as South Africa attacked Cuvelai, just as Angola did after the attack on Cangamba […] We dispatched a thousand more men to Angola [...] we applied for urgent additional supplies of arms, tanks and MiG-23s from the Soviet Union, we dispatched some arms from Cuba. And after all this the [Angolan] government decided to negotiate [...] What do they want? To make peace with South Africa and to leave us to conduct a struggle against UNITA?

> In this case the nature of our mission in Angola is changing. It will not be justified, because our current presence enjoys sympathy, but with the departure of South Africa from Namibia our struggle against UNITA will subvert the prestige of Cuba. This will be interference in domestic affairs, and we are not colonisers [...] If South Africa leaves Namibia, we would be obliged to leave Angola within a year.

> This is not 1975. We shall save Angola, defeat UNITA. But can we be sure that the history of Egypt, Somalia, and Mozambique would not be repeated? […] We can win a war, and after that the Western countries will come, give $2 billion or $3 billion and bribe Angola.[16]

7
Aftershocks

Of course, the South Africans could not – nor ever tried – to negotiate in the name of UNITA; they also never stopped supporting Savimbi's organisation. Therefore, the insurgency went on. Indeed, emboldened by its string of successes through 1983, in early 1984 the top command of FALA ordered its 2nd Strategic Front – commanded by Brigadier Joaquín Vivana Chendovaya – to attack the town of Sumbe, a place only 270 kilometres (168 miles) south of Luanda, considered safe even by the MMCA and thus populated by – amongst others – 230 Cuban civilian construction workers and teachers (including 43 women), 38 Soviet citizens, and a number of Portuguese and Bulgarians. The obvious aim of this operation was to capture some of these and thus deliver a blow to Havana's face.

Battle of Sumbe[1]
The garrison of Sumbe – the Sumbe People's Defence United Command – consisted of a motley collection of 2nd line units, including a company each of the People's Defence Organisation (Organizçâo de Defeza Popular, ODP: a MPLA/FAPLA-controlled militia) and the Ministry of Interior, and five 'companies' of virtually unarmed local militia – or about 460 Angolan and Cuban combatants armed with the usual collection of AKMs, M-52 rifles and PPSh sub machine guns, a few RPG-7s, and a single 82mm mortar. The local HQ had made some contingency planning: a defence perimeter was established, and a few defensive positions constructed on approaches to crucial buildings. However, in total, this was far from being sufficient and nobody was patrolling the surrounding countryside.

For this operation, the 2nd Strategic Front of FALA mobilised its three regional guerrilla companies (V Congreso, Bate-Cubano and the 25th), and reinforced them by the 517th Semi-Regular Battalion – about 1,500 combatants in total, supported by a number of 60mm and 82mm mortars. These units spent much of March moving westwards until reaching a point about 60km (37 miles) outside Sumbe, from where scouts were deployed on reconnaissance – all of this entirely unobserved by the government forces. From there, the final phase of the approach was initiated, with all of the involved units reaching their starting positions late on 24 March 1984. A three-pronged assault was initiated early the following morning, after a short preparatory mortar bombardment: as expected, it achieved complete surprise, and the insurgents quickly reached the

centre of the town. However, the Cubans were quick to organise themselves, and thus a series of vicious firefights erupted all over the place, stalling further FALA advances. Indeed, after several hours, the insurgents began to withdraw, taking with them 10 Portuguese and Bulgarians as hostages.

To say this attack stirred the proverbial hornet's nest would be an understatement. Minutes after being informed about the assault on Sumbe, at 07.00hrs in the morning, the MMCA set up a forward HQ in Benguela, and then launched a rescue operation including the GT from Lobito, and the Cuban Airborne Brigade from Huambo. Although marred by endemic mechanical failures of their tanks and trucks, the two units reached positions about 35km (22 miles) from Sumbe by the afternoon. Meanwhile, the DAA/FAR deployed four MiG-21s to Huambo: together with Mi-8s forward deployed at Benguela, they flew several reconnaissance sorties to assess the situation on the ground. Thanks to the barren local landscape, and despite lack of communication with ground units in the town, by 08.40hrs, the situation was clear enough for the jets to fly their first air strikes, while Mi-8s deployed 58 airborne troops to reinforce the garrison. After tracking the retreating insurgents for several hours, the Cubans then prepared a vertical envelopment operation, and deployed three groups of airborne troops along the expected routes of withdrawal. However, by cautiously manoeuvring his units, Chedonvaya managed to evade. The attack on Sumbe thus ended in a draw: while the government in Luanda, FAPLA and the MMCA were all taken aback by UNITA's capability to operate such a large force in this part of Angola, the insurgents were beaten into a hasty retreat well short of their aim, and then subjected to a total of 71 air strikes that caused them additional casualties. Overall, FALA lost 42 killed during this battle. In attempt to avenge this, UNITA then detonated a car bomb near a building housing Cubans in Huambo on 19 April 1984, killing at least 55 and wounding 63.[2]

The Switch
To say that the aftershocks of the Battles of Cangamba and Sumbe effected changes of strategic proportions would be an understatement. Before the showdown in Cangamba, Moscow limited its arms sales to Angola to vintage designs from the 1950s, such as T-54/55s, M-46 guns, and minor quantities of old jets like MiG-17Fs, MiG-21MF and MiG-21PFMs. Designed for fighting a massive conventional

One of the Soviet An-12 transports deployed to Angola on the insistence of Colonel-General Konstantin Kurochkin, in order to provide logistical support for FAPLA's offensive operations. (via Albert Grandolini)

war in Europe, and aged, this equipment was of low mechanical reliability: even relatively simple vehicles like BRDM-2 armoured scout cars and BTR-60 armoured personnel carriers frequently failed in the unforgiving African bush. Already growingly critical, Angolan leaders were now quick to blame the Soviets for dumping obsolete armament upon them. Major Alexander Petrovich Sergeev, who served as interpreter in Angola from 1987 to 1989, observed:

The Angolans....openly accused us of not giving them new technology but equipping them with rubbish from the Second World War...[of] using them as cannon fodder to suit our own purposes. They challenged us, "Where are your Sputniks, where are your modern aircraft and long-range guns? How is it possible that you, a superpower, cannot give us guns capable of fighting against obsolete South African artillery?" This ruined our reputation ... [3]

Similarly, the Cubans became convinced that the Angolans and the Soviets were embroiling them into something closely resembling what the Vietnam War was for the USA: although 'only' about 1,000 Cuban officers and other ranks were killed in Angola by the end of 1985, Havana was highly sensitive to any losses, and perfectly aware that these could easily make its intervention unsustainable. Fidel Castro was very frank when meeting Kurochkin in Havana, in early 1984: 'In your country, the losses may be unnoticeable, but in our small country, the human losses become known and have a great effect. Therefore, we are really trying to avoid losses in Angola'.[4]

Facing such bitter complaints from both allies, Colonel-General Kurochkin came to the conclusion that UNITA had to be taken seriously; indeed, that the strategy had to be switched from defence against a possible South African invasion to a major counterinsurgency effort. Contrary to other figures in his position, Kurochkin was not only a former air force officer and veteran of the Afghanistan War, but also well-connected to the Soviet Minister of Defence and the GenStab – and thus in a position to instrument a fundamental change in the USSR's approach to Angola. Henceforth, the contradiction plaguing the war effort for years ended, and now the strategy changed to 'UNITA first'. Moreover, he was able to effect a – massive – increase in the quality and quantity of arms, equipment, supplies and advice provided to Luanda. Thanks to his

The crew of a Soviet An-12 deployed to Angola in support of FAPLA's operations against the FALA from 1983, standing in front of their mount. (via Albert Grandolini)

intervention, the complement of the SMMA rose from roughly 500 in 1982 to about 2,000 by 1988, and the number of Angolan cadets sent for training in the USSR doubled at least. Indeed, Kurochkin went as far as to start sending Angolan pilots for advanced training courses in the Soviet Union, and to order the deployment of 12 Antonov An-12 transports of the VTA in Angola (reinforced by three even bigger Ilyushin Il-76s in 1986). The importance of the latter cannot be overstated as by this time all the major roads and railways in central Angola were regularly interdicted by UNITA, and transport aircraft became the only way to haul significant amounts of supplies to forward garrisons.[5]

The result was nothing short of a complete reorganisation of FAPLA and the FAPA/DAA, initiated in November 1983: its primary architect was the newly-appointed commander of the air force, Colonel Henrique Alberto Teles Carreira 'Ike Carreira', who worked closely with the Minister of Defence, Colonel Pedro Maria Tonha 'Pedale', and the new FAPLA Chief-of-Staff, Colonel Antonio dos Santos Franca 'Ndalu'.[6]

However, as time was to show, Kurochkin proved to be a mixed blessing: he was uncompromising and did his utmost to limit

A group of young Angolan MiG-21 pilots, wearing VKK-6M high-altitude pressure suits and holding Si-9 helmets. (Albert Grandolini Collection)

A group of Angolan pilots and ground personnel, together with their Soviet advisors, in front of the MiG-21bis C-63 of the 9th RAC at Lubango AB. Notable are the two R-13M infra-red homing, air-to-air missiles installed on underwing pylons and the Angolan national colours (red, yellow and black) applied down the ruder: sometime in 1984, these were replaced by a well-known 'yin & yang' roundel, in red and black, with a yellow star. (via Albert Grandolini)

ground control. This is how the first four Cuban pilots operated the MiG-21bis during the battle of Sumbe in March 1984. On the other hand, this variant did include a slightly better RP-22 Sapfir monopulse radar, it was armed with significantly improved R-13M air-to-air missiles (ASCC/NATO-codename 'AA-2B Atoll'), and – most importantly – it had an increased internal fuel capacity. As so often, the Soviets seem not to have been entirely enthusiastic about sharing details of its true range. Correspondingly, shortly after converting all of their pilots to the new variant, in early June 1984, the Cubans ran a series of tests to determine its range under combat conditions. Early trials showed that the MiG-21bis was capable of reaching as far as 240km (150 miles) from base (the distance from Luena to Saurimo) while loaded with 1,000kg of bombs or rockets and underway at a cruise speed of 750km/h (404 knots). However, another test-flight was then undertaken from Luena to Cuango and back at only 650km/h (350 knots) and an altitude of 4,000 metres (13,123ft): on return, the jet still had about 500 litres of fuel in its tanks, theoretically leaving it a 10 minute reserve – or enabling the MiG-21bis to strike a target 370km (230 miles) away from the base. This was the most significant improvement of this variant over the older MiG-21MFs and MiG-21PFMs.[12]

Silver Bullet

Meanwhile, another new type was – at least nominally – in the process of entering service with the FAPA/DAA: in early 1983, the Soviets delivered a total of 10 Su-20M (ASCC/NATOC-codename 'Fitter-D') and 2 Su-22UMs to Angola. The Su-20M was a big and heavy fighter-bomber with variable-sweep wing, custom-tailored for ground attack and capable of hauling up to 3,000kg (6,614lbs) of ordnance at a speed of 1000km/h (621mph). Its design included massive wing fences, the lower portions of which acted as hardpoints that were nearly always occupied by 600-litre or 800-litre drop tanks. Inboard underwing pylons could carry R-13M infra-red homing air-to-air missiles for self-defence, but were more often used for the same purpose as the pair of centreline hardpoints: either for the installation of UB-16-57 or UB-32-57 pods for 57mm S-5 unguided rockets or for bombs of up to 500kg per hardpoint. Its avionics outfit was quite advanced, including the SRD-5M ranging radar, the RSBN-6S instrumental navigation system, auto-pilot, and a RWR. An undernose fairing housed the Fon-1400 laser rangefinder and target-marker, and the DISS-7 Doppler navigation radar. The aircraft had two internally installed 30mm NR-30 guns with 80 rounds each and was compatible with the radio-command-guided Kh-23M (ASCC/NATO-codename 'AS-7 Kerry') missiles. Furthermore, it could be equipped with the giant – 6.79m long and 800kg KKR-1TE pod equipped for photographic survey from low and medium altitudes by day and night, and with the SRS-7 ELINT system. The primary problem of this jet was its relatively short range and lack of performance, both of which were caused by the high fuel consumption of the Tumansky R-29 engine. Nevertheless, the Su-20M was a fast and potent strike platform with an effective combat range of nearly 1,000 km (621 miles).

The first crews for Angolan Su-20Ms were mostly drawn from the ill-fated MiG-17 squadron of the 26th RACB, but these first had to undergo conversion training in the USSR. With this process being completed only in 1984, the brand-new – and, for local circumstances: highly sophisticated – jets spent their first year in Angola parked inside a hangar at Luanda IAP. Even once the Angolan pilots and ground crews were back home, and although the type eventually proved highly-popular amongst its pilots, the Soviet advisors experienced all sorts of problems while working the 26th RACB up and making it capable of running combat operations. Quite early into their operations, the jet wearing serial number C501 overshot the runway of Luanda IAP and ended up crashing into the huts beyond its end. Although remaining intact, it suffered sufficient damage to prevent any repairs in situ and subsequently served as an instructional airframe. The unit next lost one of its two precious Su-22UM conversion trainers when the engine of the jet piloted by Captain Francisco Lopes Afonso 'Hanga' (former commander of the Angolan MiG-17 squadron) surged after ingesting smoke from S-5K rockets it fired at a simulated targets on a range in the Belas area. Hanga and his Soviet instructor pilot were left with no option but to eject. A third jet is known to have been written off during the 26th RACB's transfer to its intended home-base, Yuri Gagarin AB, when Captain Domingos Alberto Serafim 'Russo' crashed on approach in bad weather and was killed. Eventually, by the end of 1985, only four out of 12 Su-20/22s remained operational and, unsurprisingly, the unit thus saw a rather 'ephemeral' participation in the war.[13]

Reorganisation of the FAPLA[14]

The increased intake of Soviet arms also prompted a comprehensive reorganisation of the FAPLA. However, contrary to the FAPA/DAA,

Sometime in 1984, Su-20M C-501 of the 26th RACB, FAPA/DAA, overshot the runway at Luanda IAP and crashed into the huts beyond, tearing away its undercarriage in the process. This photograph shows the recovery of the ill-fated jet, with the help of a heavy civilian crane. Details such as the application of the roundel of the FAPA/DAA on the fin can also be seen. (Albert Grandolini Collection)

A nice study of the right side of the Su-20M C-501, showing such details as the presence of only two centreline hardpoints under the lower centre fuselage, the application of the camouflage pattern, and the dark red serial number. (Albert Grandolini Collection)

A view from the opposite side, enabling the front section of C-501 to be seen, including obvious damage to the lower intake lip. (Albert Grandolini Collection)

A group of Angolan ground technicians – advised by two Soviet instructors – in the process of preparing Su-20M serial number C504 for a reconnaissance sortie. Visible under the centreline of the jet is the giant KKR-1 reconnaissance pod. Also visible behind is the sole Su-22UM that survived the introduction to service of this type, serial number I30. (via Albert Grandolini)

the total number of its regular units remained the same: instead, the army activated additional independent support formations – foremost artillery groups and tank battalions – which were used to bolster the fire-power of other units, as necessary. Once again, lack of personnel proved a major hindrance, and thus the most notable formations of this kind came into being only between 1986 and 1988, in the form of ground artillery brigades, including:

- 68th Ground Artillery Brigade (265th Artillery Group with D-30 howitzers, and 273rd Reactive Artillery Battery with BM-21s)
- 71st Ground Artillery Brigade (271st Reactive Artillery Group with BM-21s and a battery of D-30s)
- 80th Ground Artillery Brigade (80th Artillery Group with M-46 guns, 280th Artillery Group with A-19 guns, and 217th Reactive Artillery Group with BM-21s)

However, the build-up of 1983-1985 focused mainly on improving COIN capabilities. Correspondingly, new light infantry brigades (BrILs), with a nominal complement of 1,712 officers and other ranks, came into being. While many of them were created through the reorganisation of existing units, the best-known became the newly established 29th Airborne Brigade, which consisted of Portuguese-trained commando battalions. The BrILs operated new tactics, too, the essence of which was methodical infiltration of insurgent-controlled areas, with the aim of rooting out UNITA sympathisers. Subsequently, FAPLA sought to regain control over the local population through setting up fortified villages to keep the insurgents away.

By 1985, this strategy was applied in almost all of Angola – in turn necessitating further expansion of available manpower. The solution was found in the form of Territorial Troops, staffed by reservists. Their number increased massively, until about 158 battalions were operational in 1987, staffed by about 50,000 troops.

Ultimately, the build-up of 1983-1985 converted FAPLA into one of the biggest armed forces in Africa, counting about 193,000 officers and other ranks, supported by 300 MBTs and 400 other armoured vehicles, 1,300 guns, MRLs and mortars, and 1,000 anti-aircraft artillery pieces, MANPADs, and SAM launchers. The conventional element of the ground forces was organised into:

- 1 special forces brigade (244th)
- 2 airborne brigades (13th and 29th)

- 2 motorised infantry brigades (1st and 2nd)
- 3 artillery brigades (68th, 71st, and 80th)
- 3 air defence brigades
- 8 infantry brigades
- 43 light infantry brigades

Table 9: Known FAPLA brigades of 1983-1989	
Designation	Notes
1st BrIM	est. 1977-1980
2nd BrIM	est. 1977-1980
3rd BrI	est. 1977-1980
4th BrIL	Active as of 1982
5th BrI	est. 1977-1980
8th BrI	est. 1977-1980
9th BrIM	est. 1975, dissolved 1977
10th BrI	est. 1977-1980, converted into BrIL by 1985
11th BrI	est. 1977-1980
13th BrI	est. 1977-1980, converted into BrDA in 1983
16th BrI	est. 1977-1980
18th BrI	est. 1977-1980, converted into BrDA in 1983
19th BrI	est. 1977-1980
21st BrI	est. 1977-1980
25th BrI	N/A
29th BrDA	est. 1985, attached to the Presidency
30th BrIL	Active as of 1983
31st BrIL	Active as of 1980
32nd BrI	est. 1977-1980, converted into BrIL by 1982
33rd BrIL	est. by 1985
34th BrIL	est. by 1985
35th	est. by 1985, status uncertain, may have been BrI or BrIL
36th BrIL	est. 1977-1980
37th BrIL	est. by 1985
39th BrIL	est. by 1980
41st BrIL	est. in 1985 with battalions formerly attached to "Plan Ferro"
42nd BrIL	est. by 1985
43rd BrIL	est. by 1985
44th BrIN	est. in 1982 as "intervention" unit, converted in BrIL in 1984
45th BrIL	est. by 1980
46th BrIL	est. in 1985
47th BrIM	est. by 1987, disestablished the same year
48th BrIL	est. 1977-1980
49th BrIL	est. by 1985
50th BrIL	est. by 1984
51st BrIL	est. by 1985
52nd BDAA	anti-aircraft mobile missile systems, est. 1986, also known as "OSA-K Brigade"
53rd BrIL	est. 1977-1980
54th BrI	est. 1977-1980, converted into BrIL by 1983

Table 9: Known FAPLA brigades of 1983-1989	
Designation	Notes
55th BrIL	est. by 1986
56th BrIL	est. by 1985
57th BrIL	est. by 1982, re-designated as 100th BrIL in 1982; new 57th BrIL est. in 1985
58th BrIL	est. by 1985
59th BrIM	est. 1985-1986, disestablished 1988
60th BrIL	est. 1978-1980, re-designated as 167th BrIL 1982; new 60th BrIL est. in 1985
62nd BrIL	est. by 1984
63rd BrIL	est. by 1985
64th BrIL	est. by 1986
65th BrIL	est. by 1985
67th BrI	est. 1977-1980, converted into BrIL by 1982
68th	artillery brigade, est. in 1986
70th BrIL	est. 1977-1980
71st	artillery brigade, est. in 1986
74th BrIL	est. by 1984
75th BrIL	est. by 1985
80th	artillery brigade, Est. in 1986
81st BrIL	est. by 1985
82nd BrIL	est. by 1982
84th BrIL	re-designated as 98th BrIL in 1982; new 84th BrIL est. in 1984
86th BrIL	re-designated as 166th BrIL in 1982; new 86th BrIL est. in 1984
95th BrIL	est. by 1984
97th BrIL	est. by 1984
98th BrIL	former 84th BrIL, re-designated in 1982
100th BrIL	former 57th BrIL re-designated in 1982
143rd	mixed missiles and AAA brigade, est. in 1986
150th BrIL	est. by 1983
166th BrIL	former 86th BrIL re-designated in 1982
167th BrIL	former 60th BrIL re-designated in 1982
179th BrIL	est. by 1983
244th BrDE	est. 1986, special forces, equivalent to Soviet Spetsnaz

Endless List of Problems

Where no amount of advanced Soviet equipment could help were issues like training, supplies, and even proper treatment of the FAPLA troops – and even FAPA/DAA's helicopter crews. Indeed, the expansion of 1983-1985 proved a mixed blessing. No doubt, it was accompanied by efforts to improve training, but the mass of Angolan infantry troops were recruited forcibly, and then sent into combat after only 45 days of basic training instead of the previous 90 days. Another – and then principal – flaw was the growing gap between officers and lower ranks, and indeed: mishandling of troops by their officers, and the mistreatment of helicopter crews, which flew most of the combat sorties and suffered horrendous casualty rates, but were never as well-regarded or as respected as fighter-pilots or those operating transport aircraft.[15]

A photo from one of the training jumps of the 29th Airborne Brigade, FAPLA, taken from the rear loading ramp of one of FAPA/DAA's An-26s. This Spetsnaz-type unit was trained by the Portuguese but saw only little action during the war against UNITA and the South Africans in the 1980s. (via Tom Cooper)

Such issues had plagued FAPLA ever since 1976. Igor Zhdarkin, a Soviet interpreter serving in Angola from 1986 until 1988, recalled:

A battalion commander told me, "It is necessary to convince our soldiers, right from the start, that they are scum and good for nothing, and once this is done, they should be beaten!" Surprised, I asked him, "Do you beat your soldiers?". His reply was, "But, what should I do with them otherwise? They're just a bunch of pigs. You give them an order and they do not carry it out. Well, give them some political training – they love that – and give them political consciousness – but by making them aware they are shit. Insist that if they do not carry out their tasks, or did something else badly, or you are going to hit them in the face.[16]

Issues of this kind were further aggravated by endemic logistical problems and widespread corruption. Ever since forcing UNITA out of central and southern Angola in 1976, the mass of FAPLA units found themselves at the end of overstretched logistical arteries. Forces attempting to advance into insurgent-controlled areas after 1978 nearly always found themselves cut off from their supply bases as the insurgency systematically targeted their communication lines. Ever more often, units had to be resupplied from the air, as any attempt to do so by road required disproportionally massive effort to protect the movement of supply convoys. This had dramatic consequences for the average FAPLA trooper, as recalled by Oleg

Arkadyvich Gritsuk, a Soviet advisor assigned to the 25th BrIL: 'Daily food rations for Angolan troops were very meagre. They included 100-200 grams of rice, 60 grams of sardines, 20 grams of condensed milk, and a couple of biscuits. Had they provided so little of such food to our army, everybody would have starved within two months.'[17]

Vyacheslav Aleksandrovich Mityaev, a Soviet advisor assigned to a FAPLA reconnaissance battalion operational in the 6th Military Region, added: 'The FAPLA was fed from local sources. From 1985, this was primarily tinned food provided through humanitarian aid. UNITA was far better supplied: when our troops captured some, they would find them supplied with chocolate, pâtés, tinned ham and sausages.'[18]

What certainly failed to help improve the situation was the poor COIN tactics, foremost the slow pace of operations, as described by Gritsuk:

The 25th Brigade of FAPLA was… specialised in raiding. Its task was to destroy UNITA units. We would first identify the location of the nearby enemy unit, then would spend two weeks advancing through the savannah. During my tour of duty there, not once did we encircle any enemy base or destroy some UNITA unit. The entire war consisted of our brigade crawling along in two columns: tanks in front, and behind them trundling trucks.[19]

Overall the result was widespread defections: by 1984, these reached such proportions that the mass of light infantry brigades possessed just 30-60% of their nominal manpower at any given moment. Unsurprisingly, their actual combat effectiveness was greatly reduced.[20] Indeed, even the strength of 'elite' formations varied considerably – if only because most of them were frequently reinforced by battalion-sized independent units. For example, by 1986 the 2nd BrIM, one of best FAPLA outfits, included two tank battalions (22 MBTs each), a reconnaissance company equipped with BMP-1s and BRDM-2s, and an artillery group with D-30s and BM-21s, while its anti-aircraft defences included eight SA-13s and ZU-23s – for a total of 3,000 officers and other ranks. This, however, was an exception: the mass of infantry brigades rarely reached even 1,500 troops in total, and while they usually had an intact tank complement, virtually all their other elements were existent on paper only. This had particularly severe consequences for the BrIs, where foot-infantry was supported by much too small a truck-park, although such would have been necessary to carry at least heavy weapons, ammunition and supplies. In turn, and despite a massive investment, the truck-park of the entire FAPLA was in a sad state: cross-country operations in unforgiving African bush were tearing apart the vehicles, the mass of which were never meant to be operated in such terrain and climate. They thus needed almost permanent maintenance and repairs, which in turn greatly slowed down every advance. This issue was further aggravated by the fact that FAPLA officers were trained to react to every appearance of the enemy: every small, even indirect attack prompted them to stop and plaster the suspected enemy position with artillery and rocket fire, before resuming the advance.[21]

Overall, the massive build-up of 1983-1985 was actually counterproductive: the sheer size of the FAPLA denied the force of quality, capacity, and capability, while becoming unsustainable for an already fragile economy, which was chronically short on skilled manpower. As much as 46-47% of the annual national budget was spent for defence purposes in the mid-1980s: nevertheless, constant raids by UNITA begun delivering blows against critical civilian

Operation FAPLA 10 Years of Victories

To add salt to the wounds of UNITA, the senior leadership of FAPLA – and their Soviet advisors – was quick in organising a new offensive. After concentrating ten brigades and a commando battalion within the area of responsibility of the 3rd Military Region, and stocking enough supplies, they initiated Operation FAPLA 10 Years of Victories on 25 August 1984. Once again, two task forces advanced on Cazombo and Lumbala, respectively: however, this time also a third task force was deployed from the 6th Military Region, from Cuito Cuanavale on Mavinga. Moreover, all the known insurgent bases and defence positions along the axes of advance were subjected to an unprecedented aerial offensive, primarily by MiG-21bis. As usual, FALA offered bitter and skilful resistance. However, it proved unable to outmatch superior firepower and suffered hundreds of casualties. Arguably, Operation FAPLA 10 Years of Victories eventually experienced the same fate as most other similar offensives of the Angolan armed forces: delayed by constant ambushes and harassment attacks, it bogged down by mid-September 1984, and ultimately failed to reach its objectives. However, it caused devastating loses to the insurgents. While UNITA subsequently acknowledged only 74 of their own killed and 370 wounded, the fact was that the combat power of its 1st Strategic Front was completely demolished, and its momentum broken: this was something no amount of South African support could change for the next five years.[3]

Floggers

The two offensives run by FAPLA in eastern Angola of May-July 1984 were to be the last to see the MiG-21 acting as the backbone of both the DAA/FAR contingent and the FAPA/DAA. The process that was about to change this began almost a year earlier: indeed, deliveries of MiG-21bis to Angola had not even started when nobody less than Fidel Castro began influencing both Colonel-General Kurochkin and the ailing Soviet Leader Yuri Andropov to provided an even more advanced interceptor. Affected by the two MiG-21 losses from 1981 and 1982, and due to the requirement to establish aerial superiority over the battlefield to enable major

A still from a Cuban documentary, offering a good view of the front section of the MiG-21bis C362. Notable is the unpainted canopy frame: due to the poor quality of the Soviet-made plexiglass, constant exposure to the elements, and because the Soviets were not delivering 'spare parts' like transparancies or canopy frames, but only complete sub-assemblies (like canopy frames *with* transparancies), these required frequent replacement. (via Tom Cooper)

offensives against UNITA in south-eastern Angola, the Cuban leader demanded that Moscow deliver the Mach 2.3-capable MiG-25 interceptors (ASCC/NATO-codename 'Foxbat'), or the latest Soviet air superiority fighter, the MiG-29 (ASCC/NATO-codename 'Fulcrum'). The Soviet leadership flatly turned down both requests but agreed to provide 48 MiG-23MLs (ASCC/NATO-codename 'Flogger').

Although never as famous in the West as the MiG-25 and/or MiG-29, the MiG-23ML brought unprecedented qualities to the FAPA/DAA. The original MiG-23 was designed as a high-speed interceptor capable of reaching speeds of more than Mach 2 and of destroying low-flying targets, but with minimal capabilities in manoeuvring air combat. Early variants suffered from poor avionics, low manufacturing quality, and their export variants earned themselves an awful reputation in the Middle East. However, the Soviets invested heavily into refining the type: the result was the MiG-23ML – probably the finest variant of this prolific family, with much improved air combat capabilities and manoeuvrability,

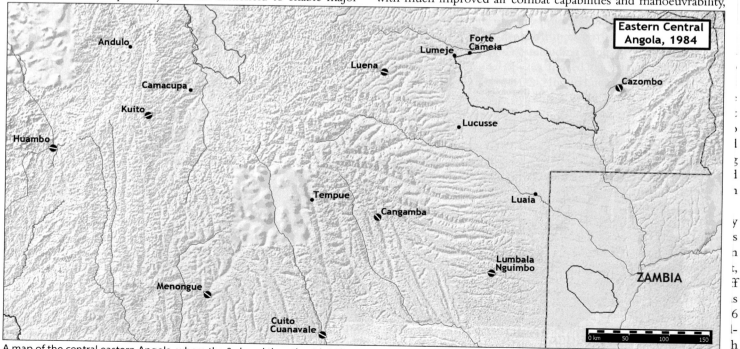

A map of the central eastern Angola, where the 3rd, and then the 6th Military Regions of FAPLA ran their first two major offensives against FALA, in May-August 1984. (Map by Tom Cooper)

and a quality entirely unknown in the West in the mid-1980s. Not without some bitterness, the Cubans accepted – and the Angolans agreed to pay. The first batch of 12 MiG-23ML reached Lubango AB by May 1984, followed by two MiG-23UB two-seat conversion trainers. Correspondingly, most of the MiG-21 pilots of the DAA/FAR contingent started their conversion training on the new type, supported by members of the SMMA.[4]

Although still equipped with relatively austere avionics, and heavily reliant on the ground control for effective operation, except if used with the RSBN (which, as described above: was useless in Angola due to the lack of ground-based radio beacons), the MiG-23ML came in the form of a light-weight airframe stressed for accelerations up to 8.5g. It was powered by the improved Tumansky R-35F-300 engine and equipped with an inertial navigation system (INS) with an autopilot, the SPO-15L radar warning receiver, and the RP-23M Sapfir III radar. If well-maintained and calibrated, the latter had a maximum detection range for fighter-sized targets underway at medium and high altitudes of 65km (35 miles) and could track (or 'lock on' to) a target inside 35km (22 miles) – which was the maximum range for the primary weapon of this variant, the Vympel R-24R semi-active radar homing (SARH) air-to-air missile (ASCC/NATO-codename 'AA-7C Apex') – from all aspects. Perhaps more importantly for Angolan circumstances, while a pulse radar with analogue processing, the Sapfir III used pulse-doppler techniques to give reasonably good look-down/shoot-down capability: i.e. the ability to target low-flying aircraft. In such a working mode, it could engage with R-24Rs out to a range of 11km (6.8 miles). Continuously developed during the 1970s and 1980s, the sub-variant delivered to Angola used a large number of doppler filters to improve its ability to pick up low-flying targets from the rear hemisphere – as when the MiG was chasing its opponent. Still, as a back-up for such operations, the MiG-23ML was further equipped with the TP-23ML infra-red search and track system (IRST), which enabled the deployment of the infra-red homing R-24T missile. Finally, the RP-23 had an air combat mode, custom-tailored for short-range combat, in which the radar automatically locked-on to the first target that entered its envelope out to a range of 9km (5nm). For such short-range engagements the MiG-23ML was armed with the R-60MK (ASCC/NATO-codename 'AA-8 Aphid') infra-red homing air-to-air missile, which could be aimed with the help of the radar, the TP-23ML IRST, or the optical gun-sight. With this wide range of new capabilities, the MiG-23ML completely outclassed the Mirage F.1AZ/CZ of the SAAF – and also did so in terms of power and acceleration, manoeuvrability, and firepower.[5]

Peculiarities of the MiG-23
The most notable outside difference between the MiG-23 and older Soviet-made jets was that – like the Su-20M – it was a variable-geometry aircraft: it could sweep it wings back and then return them to their original straight position depending on the flight regime. To keep the swing-wing mechanism simple, this was operated by the pilot, who could re-position the wings in one of four positions: 16, 45, 55 and 72 degrees. A little-known result was that depending on the wing-sweep, the MiG-23 could behave like four different aircraft. Trjujillo Hernández described it as follows:

> With wings at 16 degrees, the MiG-23 was a very docile aircraft, with good manoeuvrability. The wing position at 45 degrees was used for air combat or bombing runs….it felt like flying a MiG-15 or MiG-17, but with a much more powerful engine. With wings set at 55 degrees, the aircraft behaved like the MiG-21,

and at 72 degrees, it had a tremendous acceleration and speed…. [the] Main problem was that the pilot had to master all of these performances on one aircraft.[6]

Unsurprisingly – and while the MiG-23 offered much improved range in comparison to earlier models, and was a robust aircraft capable of operations from short and primitive runways made of compressed soil – mastering it was a challenge. Working under immense pressure from Havana to make their new MiG-23MLs operational as soon as possible, the DAA/FAR contingent pressed the type into action in a great rush while lacking the necessary ground support. The consequences this could have became obvious during the first known combat operation involving MiG-23s.

Early on 8 September 1984, the Cuban COMINT services detected the presence of Jonas Savimbi at a rally held near the town of Lumbala Nguimbo, in the far east of Angola. The Cubans scrambled to exploit the opportunity, and two MiG-23MLs standing quick reaction alert at Lubango AB were prepared to attack this rally in an attempt to assassinate the insurgent leader. The principal problem for their mission was distance: situated about 60km (37 miles) west of the border with Zambia, the target (which had a small airstrip nearby) was no less than 855km (531 miles) away from Lubango – well beyond the reach of the MiG-23ML. Theoretically, this variant could reach such distances by using underwing drop tanks (which had to be ejected before the pilot could swing the wing from the full-forward position and go into combat). However, out of fear that the Cubans might use their new mounts to fly strikes on SAAF air bases in South West Africa, Moscow refused to deliver any (and continued to refuse delivering any well into 1988). Therefore, the Cubans had no option but to transfer their jets to Luena on the way in, even if this meant that they would probably lose the moment of surprise: this airfield was still 305km (168 miles) from the target, but this would mean that the pilots would have to fly the final part of the mission over a much shorter range.[7]

The formation sent on this mission consisted of four aircraft, each loaded with one FAB-500M-62 bomb under each wing, and a single drop tank under the centreline. The leader was Major Antonio Rojas Marrero: he piloted a MiG-23UB two-seater (probably serial number I22), with Colonel Jorge Villadrel – who knew the region from earlier operations there – in the rear cockpit. On Rojas Marrero's wing was Lieutenant Alberto Pérez Pérez in a MiG-23ML. The other two MiG-23MLs were piloted by Captain Pedro Zequeiras Moreno and Lieutenant Juan Alberto Olivares Horta. Although launched in a great rush, and poorly-prepared, the formation crossed almost the full width of Angola on the way in, refuelled at Luena, and then launched again: they found their target and dropped bombs on the meeting in Lumbala Nguimbo without disruption. While it is certain that Savimbi came away, it remains unknown what kind of damage was caused. However, this was when the problems of the five Cuban pilots began. While the mission was underway, the P-12 radar in Luena malfunctioned: with the local airfield having no other radio navigation equipment, this meant that the ground control could neither detect nor guide the four fighters on their way back. Indeed, it is known that only a few days earlier an An-26 carrying General Cintra Frias – the head of the MMCA – got lost while trying to reach this airfield, even though without consequences thanks to the aircraft's good range. This was not to be the case for the four MiG-23s – all of which were now desperately short on fuel.[8]

One way or the other, Rojas Marrero eventually found Luena airport, but came in with too much speed, overshot on approach

What's in the Flogger?

Ever since the Korean War, and also during and after the Angolan War of 1975-1992, there has been no end of debate about Soviet and Western combat aircraft – and fighter jets in particular. Their performances have been discussed in thousands of studies by professionals and enthusiasts alike, and there are no end of disputes about the supposed superiority of one or the other model, and its equipment. However, 30 years – and thousands of related publications – later, several conclusions become obvious. The primary amongst these is that the threat perceptions driving the development of Soviet combat aircraft in service during the 1970s and the 1980s were entirely different than those of the West. Indeed, that understanding them requires putting oneself into the Soviets' shoes.

Combat experience from the Korean War had its influences, but what impressed the Soviets the most during that war were the US-made bombers, and the devastation these caused to North Korea. Moreover, back in the late 1940s and most of the 1950s, the huge Soviet airspace was regularly penetrated by all sorts of US and British reconnaissance aircraft, especially those flying high and fast proved beyond the reach of the available Soviet interceptors. Moreover, the Soviets knew that the USA, Great Britain and France were developing even more advanced, ever higher and faster-flying bombers, many of these equipped with cruise missiles. The conclusion reached was that the Soviet Air Force (Voyenno-Vozdushnye Sily, V-VS), and especially the Air Defence Force (Voyska Protivovozdushnoy Oborny, V-PVO) had to be equipped with an extensive radar network capable of early detection of any kind of intruders, a command, control, and communication system enabling quick reaction, with manned interceptors capable of not only catching, but actually destroying any intruder – and then as quickly as possible (preferably before any incoming bombers could release their nuclear-tipped missiles). As a result, Soviet interceptors had to fly ever faster and higher, and to be armed with large air-to-air missiles, necessary to ascertain the destruction of any target with a single blow. Unsurprisingly, the starting point for research and development of types like the MiG-17 and MiG-21 was the 'defence of the Rodina' (Soviet homeland): they were to become the 'spear tip' of a complex IADS protecting the whole Soviet airspace, and especially major urban centres and military installations.

Then, in the late 1950s and early 1960s, the V-PVO introduced to service a large number of SA-2 SAM systems, which quickly proved capable of intercepting even high-flying Lockheed U-2 reconnaissance jets. The appearance of the SA-2 – and subsequent, even longer-ranged and more advanced SAM systems – forced the Western strategists to change the way they intended to fight a war against the USSR, and switch the tactics of their bomber forces to low-altitude operations. Around 1960, NATO began purchasing thousands of Lockheed F-104G Starfighters, and the US

Two Cuban pilots (including Albert Rey Rivas) in front of the MiG-23UB serial I21 in the mid-1980s. (Verde Olivo via Luis Dominguez)

Air Force began acquiring Republic F-105 Thunderchiefs, and then later General Dynamics F-111s – all of which were custom-tailored for high-speed operations at low altitudes. Preoccupied with preparing the Soviet armed forces for an all-out war against NATO, the list of the GenStab's priorities thus grew immensely: in the worst case, it now had to equip the V-VS and the V-PVO with the capability of intercepting literally thousands of low-flying aircraft carrying nuclear bombs. Under such circumstances, there was no margin for error and no time to waste thinking about air combat against nimble fighters: the priority was to detect, intercept and kill whatever the incoming target was, before it could vaporise anything with its nuclear bomb.

Such threat perceptions led to several conclusions. All command, control, and communication functions (C3) had to be strictly centralised. Potential targets were expected to be detected by the C3 system, supported by a well-developed radar network and input from all other available sensors, intelligence services, and visual observation posts. The HQ of the C3 system was then to scramble its interceptors, guide one or two of them against

Crews of the first Cuban MiG-23 squadron, together with Angolan troops that protected Lubango AB, shortly before the Cuban withdrawal in 1989. The jet visible here was the MiG-23UB two-seat conversion trainer wearing the serial I21: it was one of three used to convert DAA/FAR's pilots to the MiG-23MLs since 1984. (Verde Olivo via Pit Weinert)

every single one of the expected targets along ideal intercept vectors, enable them to acquire with on-board sensors, and to quickly kill with a single blow. Such operations required no wasting of time or fuel with flying combat air patrols, tedious searches for targets with on-board sensors, or with dogfighting: they also provided an advantage because the Soviets began to lag behind the West in regards of advanced technologies and miniaturisation, both of which were related to excessive cost – which was something the USSR could not afford. Correspondingly, instead of installing thousands of computers into thousands of aircraft, the Soviets concluded it a cheaper and simpler idea to install computers into individual headquarters, in turn enabling their commanders to run the battle, essentially by remote control.

It can be said, that by thinking this way the military theoreticians of the GenStab had reduced aerial warfare to its lowest common denominator. The fighters required no complex and expensive avionics, and only needed carry enough fuel and weapons for a quick and decisive execution of their task. This was the design philosophy that resulted in the MiG-21, and then was driven to the extreme in the case of MiG-23 and MiG-25.

The very same design philosophy resulted in the emergence of two variants of the same type of air-to-air missiles: one semi-active radar homing (SARH) and the other infra-red homing (IRH). While Western analysts

were wondering about all the supposed 'advantages' of such a combination, the simple fact was that Soviet-made pulse-Doppler radars of the late 1960s and the early 1970s – including the Sapfir-23ML – were relatively good at detecting and tracking incoming targets, but, for reasons of simplicity, either had a very limited, or entirely lacking, capability to detect and track targets moving away, or flying at co-speed. Correspondingly, types like the MiG-23 were supposed to use their SARH air-to-air missiles for intercepts from the front aspect, and infra-red homing missiles in pursuit. Alternatively, infra-red homing missiles were to act as a 'spare' weapon, in the event that the SARH missile failed to hit or destroy the target.

It was only during the early 1970s that the Soviets – on basis of Arab and North Vietnamese combat experiences – concluded that the early versions of the MiG-23 lacked the 'second attack capability': that they were too poorly manoeuvrable, if their first attack failed, to turn around and re-attack. This is what prompted not only the development of the more manoeuvrable (in comparison to early MiG-23, MiG-23S, and MiG-23M variants) MiG-23ML, and advanced air-to-air missiles with the capability of tracking targets at high off-boresight angles: thus came into being the R-60, which was expected to enable less manoeuvrable MiGs to target nimble enemy fighters. In the USSR, this entered service in 1973: the first examples reached Angola together with the first batch of MiG-23MLs.

A pair of brand-new MiG-23MLs (visible in the centre is the example with serial C428), in front of one of the hardened aircraft shelters housing aircraft kept on quick reaction alert, at Lubango AB. (Albert Grandolini Collection)

A still from a video showing a MiG-23UB taking off from Lubango AB for a training sortie. Notably, the jet was armed with R-13M air-to-air missiles: however, two-seat conversion trainers were considered precious assets, and thus rarely deployed in combat. (Tom Cooper Collection)

For comparison, this photograph shows an FAPA/DAA MiG-23ML (all of which were still flown by Cuban pilots as of 1984), carrying a full complement of air-to-air missiles, including an R-24T (the big white missile on the underwing hardpoint nearest to the camera), and two R-60MKs (installed on hardpoints low on the fuselage, either side of the drop tank). (Verde Olivo)

and went for another landing attempt. While circling the runway, his aircraft ran out of fuel, the engine quit working, and the crew was forced to eject. Alberto Pérez then manged to land safely. Meanwhile, the pilots of the rear pair of MiG-23MLs – Zequeirras Moreno and Olivares Horta – lost visual contact with the front pair, and then also ran out of fuel. Eventually, both were forced to make emergency landings on a dirt track outside the deserted village named 'Marimba' (not to be confused with the town in Marimba, northern Angola, next to the border with Zaire), about 60 kilometres west of Luena – and thus deep within a territory swarming with insurgents. Both jets suffered some engine damage due to the sand and dirt sucked through intakes during landing, but were otherwise perfectly intact.[9]

Fortunately for Zequeirras Moreno and Olivares Horta, there were still eight Mi-8 and five Mi-25 helicopters at Luena airport, from Operation FAPLA 10 Years of Victories. These were promptly sent to search for the two missing airmen, followed by two MiG-21bis from Menongue. Eventually, they managed to find Zequeirras Moreno and Olivares Horta, but one MiG-21bis also ran out of fuel and Captain Pausides Heredia Hechevaria crash-landed in the Cuemba area. Ultimately, the Cubans had to deploy their special forces to extract all three pilots: they destroyed all three jets to prevent them from falling into insurgent hands (or, worse yet: into South African hands), and then evacuated the pilots into the waiting Mi-8s.[10]

Radar Core to the Rescue

To say that this experience provoked another bitter confrontation between the Cubans and Kurochkin would be an understatement. Officers of the MMCA could not stop complaining about the weak spots of the Soviet-made aircraft and the Soviet refusal to provide underwing drop tanks for MiG-23MLs – although they should have known that their own pilots had flown the same mission in much shorter-ranged MiG-21MFs as early as 1976, and without any problems. In turn, Kurochkin

The wreckage of one of two MiG-23MLs landed by Captain Pedro Zequeira and Lieutenant Alberto Olivares Horta after the failed attempt to attack a rally visited by Savimbi, on 8 September 1984 – as found by FALA insurgents. Notably, the jet wore no Angolan national marking yet, and its entire front section (including all sensitive equipment) was completely destroyed by the Cuban special forces that evacuated Zequeira and Horta. (Al J Venter Collection)

could only answer that Moscow did everything in its power to help. Arguably, the Soviets were right: through 1983 and 1984, they delivered 68 MiG-21bis, 12 MiG-23MLs, 12 Su-20/22s, 24 Mi-25s, plus 12 Strela-10M and Strela-3 SAM-systems, and up to 4,000 SA-7 MANPADs to Angola.[11] Indeed, the ranks of the 9th RAC were further reinforced in December 1984 when 10 Angolan pilots returned from a conversion course for MiG-21s in the USSR. The FAPA/DAA and the DAA/FAR contingents were thus bolstered to a total of 115 aircraft and helicopters, 92 of which were jet fighters (86 of which were still operational as of August 1984).[12]

The problem was that this

Crew of the 24th BDAA installing a new missile on one of six SM-63 launchers of their Combat Group. (Albert Grandolini Collection)

was still not enough: not only had the SAAF deployed 150 combat aircraft during Operation Protea, for example, but the experience of 8 September 1984 had shown that Soviet aircraft required much more ground support equipment to be operated effectively. Eventually, a solution was found in the Angolans and their allies once again intensifying the expansion of the 'radar core' of the FAPA/DAA. This proved impossible in the short term: although dozens of additional Angolan cadets were now undergoing training in the USSR, the sole immediate solution was to deploy additional DAA/FAR-personnel to Angola. Correspondingly, in addition to manning most of the two missile brigades of the Angolan air defences, additional Cuban officers and other ranks were brought in to man additional equipment organised into the 1st and 2nd Radar Battalions. When these two units operated about 50 different systems – meanwhile deployed outside every major urban centre of southern Angola – they were expanded into two Regiments of Radio-Technical Troops (Regimento de Tropas Rádio Técnicas, RTRTs), each of which consisted of about ten groups of radio-technical troops. Similarly, FAPLA exploited the opportunity to expand its air defence assets: due to the shortage of suitable personnel, it began converting infantry into anti-aircraft artillery units to create about a dozen new anti-aircraft groups. Finally, in order to expand

the range of their air defences, the Angolans demanded – and the Soviets delivered – one S-75M Volga and three S-75M Volkhov SAM systems (ASCC/NATO-codenamed 'SA-2C Guideline'). These became the primary armament of the 24th BDAA of the FAPA/DAA, organised into Combat Groups 1-3 (each of which operated one SAM site with six launchers). While longer-ranged than the SA-3, the SA-2 proved easier to re-deploy, but lacked the flexibility and capability to counter low-flying targets. Therefore, single combat groups of the 24th BDAA were always combined

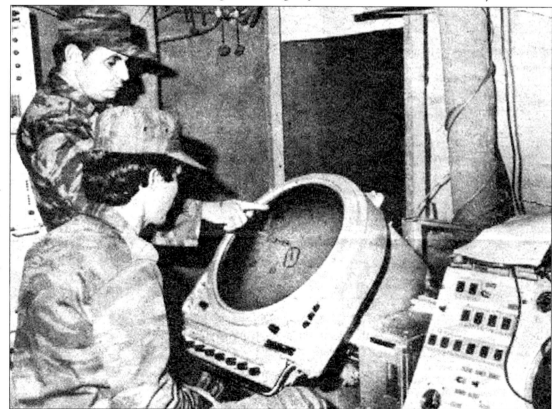

A Soviet advisor with one of the Angolan radar operators: a well-developed radar network proved of crucial importance for the proper function of the entire FAPA/DAA. Correspondingly, the Angolans, Cubans, and the Soviets invested massively into the built-up of the Angolan radar units. (Albert Grandolini Collection)

Table 10: FAPA/DAA, ORBAT, late 1985[14]

Element	HQ	Equipment
RA/DAAN	HQ Luanda	CO Major Altino Carlos dos Santos; responsible for provinces Bengo, Benguela, Cabinda, Cuanzo North, Cuanza South, Luanda, Lunda North, Lunda South, Malanje, Uige and Zaire
1st RTRT		Total of 10 radar companies (or 'groups'), including 1 in Luanda and 1 in Saurimo
7th RATM	Luanda IAP	An-2, BN-2, 17 An-26
17 RAH	Huambo AB	20 Mi-8, 10 Mi-17, 22 Mi-25, 28 Alouette III
174th BDAA	Lobito AB	
176th BDAA	Cabinda	
190th BDAA	Soyo	
197th BDAA	Luanda IAP	
188 ENAM	Negage AB	Cessna FR-172K, IAR.823
189 ENAL	Lobito AB	IAR.316B/SE.316B
RA/DAAS	HQ Lubango	Lubango seems to have received official designation 'Air Base No. 5'
9th RAC	Lubango	47 MiG-21bis/UM, 12 MiG-23UB/ML
26th RACB	Catumbela, Yuri Gagarin/ Namibe AB	10 Su-20/22, 8 PC-7
24th BDAA	Cuando Cubango, Menongue	1 combat group with SA-2, 2 with SA-3
40th BDAA	Lubango, Cuando Cubango	1 combat group with SA-2, 3 with SA-3
213th BDAA	Xangongo, Matala	
214th BDAA	Yuri Gagarin/Namibe AB	
230th RTRT	Lubango AB	Total of 10 radar companies (or 'groups'), including 1 in Cahama and 1 in Chibemba

Table 11: FAPLA/DAA Commanders, 1976-1989[15]

Period	Rank	Name	Notes
1976-1978	Commandante	João Filipe Neto 'Dimbōndwa'	former FAPLA guerrillero, underwent elementary pilot course, but failed to graduate
1978-1982	Colonel	Ciel da Conceição Cristóvão 'Gato'	former FAPLA guerrillero
1982-1983	Colonel	António dos Santos Franca 'N'Dalu'	
1983-1987	Colonel	Henrique Teles Carreira 'Iko'	former FAPLA guerrillero
1987-1989	Lieutenant-Colonel	Alberto Correia Neto	

with combat groups operating SA-3s, to create 'mixed' BDAAs. The operation of such mixed SA-2 and SA-3 SAM-units might appear logical, but their direct integration proved impossible. Instead, they were 'integrated' at the brigade-level, through the use of the same early warning radar (usually the P-19), the crew of which distributed targets to specific units.[13]

This massive expansion of the FAPA/DAA of 1984-1985 prompted another reorganisation of the force: the Esquadron de Transportes was converted into the 7th Mixed Transport Aviation Regiment (Regimento Aéro de Transporte Misto, RATM), while the massive expansion of ground-based air defences necessitated a split of the air force into two major commands: the Northern Air Defence Region (Região Aéra e Defesa Anti-Aérea Norte, RA/DAAN), and the Southern Air Defence Region (RA/DAAS). Combined with the re-armament of the whole of FAPLA and the decision to switch the strategy to that of 'UNITA first', this was how the stage was set for an escalation of the war in Angola to unprecedented dimensions: this will be the topic of the next volume in this series.

Bibliography

Abrantes, H. C., *Enciclopédia da Aviação Militar Angolana 1975-1991* (Sinapis Editores: Lisboa, 2019)

Baxter, P., *SAAF's Border War: The South African Air Force in Combat, 1966-1989* (Warwick: Helion & Co., 2019)

Brent, W., *African Air Forces* (Nelspruit: Freeworld Publications, 1999)

Bridgland, F, *Jonas Savimbi; A Key to Africa; The Story behind the Battle for Angola* (New York: Paragon House Publishers, 1987)

Bridgland, F, *The War for Africa: Twelve Months that Transformed a Continent* (Oxford: Casemate Publishers, 2017)

Campos P, Pedro Edy & Acosta Leyva, Maricel Elena; *Bayate y la misión en Angola* (Guantanamo: Editorial El Mar y la Montaña, 2012)

Capy, X., & Millas, G., *Le Noratlas: Du Nord 2500 au Nord 2508* (Éditions Lela Presse: Collection Profils Avions No. 29)

Carreras Rolas, E., *Por El Dominio del Aire: Memorias de un piloto de combate, 1943-1988* (Havana: Editora Politica, 2008)

Choy, A., Chui, G.,ä & Sio Wong, M., *Our History is Still Being Written; the Story of Three Chinese-Cuban Generals in the Cuban Revolution* (Pathfinder Books: 2006)

Conceição, M. G. da & Ramos, J. da G., *Contribuição para a História da FAPA-DAA* (Luanda: Edições Mayamba, 2017)

Cooper, T. & Santana, S., *Lebanese Civil War, Volume 1: Palestinian Diaspora, Syrian and Israeli Interventions, 1970-1978* (Warwick: Helion & Co., 2019)

Cooper, T., *Great Lakes Holocaust: First Congo War, 1996-1997* (Solihull: Helion & Co., 2013)

Cooper, T., *Hot Skies over Yemen, Volume 1: Aerial Warfare Over the Southern Arabian Peninsula, 1962-1994* (Solihull, Helion & Co., 2017)

Cooper, T., *MiG-23 Flogger in the Middle East: Mikoyan i Gurevich MiG-23 in Service in Algeria, Egypt, Iraq, Libya, and Syria, 1973-2018* (Warwick, Helion & Co., 2019)

Cooper, T., Weinert, P, Hinz, F., & Lepko, M., *African MiGs; MiGs and Sukhois in Service in Sub-Saharan Africa; Volume 1, Angola to Ivory Coast* (Houston: Harpia Publishing, 2010)

Cooper, T., *Wings over Ogaden: The Ethiopian-Somali War, 1978-1979* (Solihull: Helion & Co., 2015)

DIA, *Handbook of the Cuban Armed Forces* (Washington DC: Defence Intelligence Agency, April 1979)

Ferreira de Oliviera, A., *A Formação dos Oficiais das Forças Armadas Angolanas* (Instituto de Estudos Superiores Militares, 2009)

Flintham, V., *Air Wars and Aircraft: A detailed Record of Air Combat, 1945 to the Present* (London: Arms and Armour Press, 1989)

Fontanellaz, A, *War of Intervention in Angola, Volume 2: Angolan and Cuban Forces at War, 1976-1983* (Warwick: Helion & Co., 2019)

Fontanellaz, A., & Cooper, T., *War of Intervention in Angola, Volume 1: Angolan and Cuban Forces at War, 1975-1976* (Warwick: Helion & Co., 2018)

Força Aérea Nacional, *História sobre a Aviação, colectânea do 1° Colóquio sobre a História da FAPA/DAA* (Luanda: Editora mayamba, 2ª edição, 2014)

Garcia, M. R., *Prisioneiros da UNITA nas Terras do Fim do Mundo* (Mayamba Editora, 2012)

George, E., *The Cuban Intervention in Angola, 1965-1991, From Che Guevara to Cuito Cuanavale* (Oxon: Frank Cass, 2005)

Gleijeses, P., *Visions of Freedom: Havana, Washington, Pretoria, and the Struggle for Southern Africa; 1976-1991* (The University of North Carolina Press, 2013)

Glória, R. da, et al, *Força Aérea Nacional; Contribuição para a História da FAPA-DAA* (Camama: Mayamba Editora, 2017)

Grau, Dr. L. W., & Bartles, C. K., *The Russian Way of War: Force Structure, Tactics and Modernization of the Russian Ground Forces* (Foreign Military Studies Office, 2016)

Green, W. & Fricker, J., *The Air Forces of the World: Their History, Development and Present Strength* (London: MacDonald, 1958)

Harmse, K. & Dunstan, S.; *South African Armour of the Border War 1975-89* (Oxford: Osprey Publishing, 2017)

Heitman, H., R., *South African War Machine* (Greenwich: Bison Books Corp., 1985)

Hernández, H. T., *Audacia Y Corage – Proezas de la aviación cubana en Angola* (Havana: Editorial de Ciencias Sociales, 2012)

Hooper, J., *Bloodsong; An Account of Executive Outcomes in Angola* (London: HarperCollins Publishers, 2002)

Jiménez Gómez, R. G., *En el sur de Angola* (La Habana: Instituto Cubano del Libro, 2009)

Junior, M., *Forças Armadas Populares de Libertação de Angola (FAPLA) – Primeiro Exército Nacional (1975-1992)* (Lisboa: Prefácio, 2007)

Junior, M., *Popular Armed Forces for the Liberation of Angola; First National Army and the War (1975-1992)* (Bloomington: Authorhouse, 2015)

Labuschagne, B., *South Africa's Intervention in Angola: Before Cuito Cuanavale and Thereafter* (Thesis, Stellenbosch University, 2009)

Lambeth, B. S., *Russia's Air Power at the Crossroads* (Santa Monica: RAND, 1996)

Liebenberg, I., Risquet, J., Shubin, V., *A Far-Away War; Angola 1975-1989* (Sun Press: 2015)

Lord, D., *From Fledgling to Eagle; the South African Air Force during the Border War* (Johannesburg: 30 Degrees South Publishers, 2008)

Lord, D., *Vlamgat; The Story of the Mirage F1 in the South African Air Force* (Johannesburg: 30 Degrees South Publishers, 2000)

Mannall, D.; *Battle on the Lomba 1987: The day a South African Armoured Battalion shattered Angola's Last Mechanised offensive – A Crew Commander's Account* (Solihull: Helion & Company Limited, 2015)

McWilliams, M., *Battle for Cassinga: South Africa's Controversial Cross-Border Raid, Angola 1978* (Warwick: Helion & Co., 2019)

Milhazes, J., *Golpe Nito Alves e Outros Momentos da História de Angola Vistos do Kremelin* (Lisboa, Alêtheia Editores, 2013)

Muekalia, J., *Angola a Segunda Revolução – Memórias da luta pela Democracia* (Porto: Sextante Editora, 4ª edição, 2013)

Nengovhela, L. J., *The Role Played by the People's Liberation Army of Namibia (PLAN) during the Namibian struggle, 1978 to 1989* (Rand Afrikaans University, 1999)

Neto, M., *História sobre a Defesa Antiaérea, Colectânea do 1° Colóquio sobre a História da FAPA/DAA* (Luanda: Mayamba Editora, 2ª edição, 2014)

Nortje, P., *The Terrible Ones; The Complete History of 32 Battalion, Volumes 1 and 2,* (Cape Town: Zebra Press, 2012)

Nujoma, S., *Where Others Wavered; The Autobiography of Sam Nujoma* (London: Panaf Books, 2001)

Oosthuizen, G., *The South African Defence Force and operation Hooper, Southeast Angola, December 1987 to March 1988* (Scientia Militaria, South African Journal of Military Studies, Vol 42, No 2, 2014)

Paulino, J. A., *História sobre a Aviação, Colectânea do 1° Colóquio sobre a História da FAPA/DAA* (Luanda: Editora Mayamba, 2ª edição, 2014)

Perez Cabrera, R., *La Historia Cubana en África* (Havana: Edição de autor, 2011; ISBN: 9781447502203)

Pino, R. del, *Los Anos de la Guerra* (Edição de autor: 2013)

Pino, R. del, *The African Adventure – A Cuban perspective of Air Operations in Angola* (online document, including English translation of del Pino's book 'Proa a Libertad', issued 2012)

Pino, R., del, *Inside Castro's Bunker* (CreateSpace Independent Publishing Platform, 2012)

Polack, P; *The Last Hot Battle of the Cold War; South Africa vs. Cuba in the Angolan Civil War* (Oxford: Casemate Publishers, 2013)

Porter, B., D., *The USSR in Third World Conflicts: Soviet Arms and Diplomacy in Local Wars 1945-1980* (Cambridge, Cambridge University Press, 1986)

Queiroz, A., *Angola do 25 de Abril ao 11 de Novembro: A Via Agreste da Liberdade* (Lisboa: Publicações Biblioteca Ulmeiro No.13, 1978)

Ramos Fajardo, R. Á., *Tigres de Cangamba* (La Habana: Casa Editorial Verde Olivo, 2015)

Ramos, J. da G., *Angola pelos Caminhos da Paz – Guerra e Diplomacia (1975-2002)* (Luanda: Mayamba Editora, 2018)

Ramos, J. da G., *Força Aérea Nacional: Contribuição para a história da FAPA-DAA* (Camama: Mayamba Editora, 2017)

Raspletin, Dr. A. A., *History PVO website* (historykpvo.narod2.ru), 2013

Salgado Méndez, L., *Angola Frente Norte* (La Havana: Casa Editorial Olivo, 2015)

Scholz, L., *The Battle of Cuito Cuanavale, Cold War Angolan Finale, 1987-1988* (Warwick: Helion & Co., 2019)

Scholz, L., *The SADF in the Border War 1966-1989* (Solihull: Helion & Company, 2015)

Shubin, G., Tokarev, A., *Bush War, The Road to Cuito Cuanavale; Soviet Soldiers' Accounts of the Angolan War* (Auckland Park: Jacana Media, 2011)

Shubin, G., Zhdarkin, I., Barabulya, V. & Kuznetsova-Timoneva, A.; *Cuito Cuanavale; Frontline Accounts by Soviet Soldiers* (Auckland Park: Jacana Media, 2014)

Shubin, V., *The Hot 'Cold War': the USSR in Southern Africa* (London: Pluto Press, 2008)

Silva, P; Esteves, F., Moreira, V., *Angola: Comandos Especiais contra os Cubanos* (Braga Editora, 1978)

About the Authors

Adrien Fontanellaz

Adrien Fontanellaz, from Switzerland, is a military history researcher and author. He developed a passion for military history at an early age and has progressively narrowed his studies to modern-day conflicts. He is a member of the Scientific Committee of the Pully-based Centre d'Histoire et de Prospective Militaires (Military History and Prospectives Centre), and regularly contributes for the Revue Militaire Suisse and various French military history magazines. This is his 11th title for Helion's @War series.

Jose Matos

José Matos is an independent researcher in military history in Portugal with a primary interest in the operations of the Portuguese Air Force during the colonial wars in Africa, especially in Guinea. He is a regular contributor to numerous European magazines on military aviation and naval subjects and has collaborated in the major project The *Air Force at the end of the Empire*, published in Portugal in 2018. He has recently written two books in Portuguese on the former regime's relations with South Africa and on the Portuguese attack on Guinea-Conakry in 1970. This is his first instalment for Helion.

Tom Cooper

Tom Cooper is an Austrian aerial warfare analyst and historian. Following a career in the worldwide transportation business – during which he established a network of contacts in the Middle East and Africa – he moved into narrow-focus analysis and writing on small, little-known air forces and conflicts, about which he has collected extensive archives. This has resulted in specialisation in such Middle Eastern air forces as of those of Egypt, Iran, Iraq, and Syria, plus various African and Asian air forces. In addition to authoring and co-authoring about 50 books – including about three dozen titles for Helion's @War series – and well over 1,000 articles. Cooper has been the editor of the five @War series since 2017, and this is his 34th book for Helion.